M000287297

Designing and Making Jewellery

Designing and Making
Jewellery

Sarah Macrae

The Crowood Press

First published in 2001 by
The Crowood Press Ltd
Ramsbury, Marlborough
Wiltshire SN8 2HR

© Sarah Macrae 2001

All rights reserved. No part of this publication may be reproduced or transmitted in any form or by any means, electronic or mechanical, including photocopy, recording, or any information storage and retrieval system, without permission in writing from the publishers.

British Library Cataloguing-in-Publication Data
A catalogue record for this book is available from the British Library.

ISBN 1 86126 427 5

Dedication
To all my family and friends for their support, patience and encouragement and to all the jewellers who kindly lent me slides of their work to illustrate this book.

Photographic Acknowledgements
All photographs by the author except for those on the following pages, the copyright of which remains with the photographers indicated:
Alison Baxter 38 (upper); Mike Blisset 34 (upper), 40 (upper), 124 (lower); Philip Booth 89 (upper); Steven Braene 31 (lower); Faith Chapman 148; Martin Cleveland (50 right); Joel Degen 8, 35, 49 (lower), 50 (left), 51 (upper), 102, 136; Robert Diamante 41, 42; Rodney Forte 86; William Guilett 30 (upper), 80, 105, 106; Frank Hills 11, 14, 39; Norman Hollands 146; Mike Inch 37 (lower), 51 (lower); EM Jewellery 88, 90, 91; Chris Lockyer 38 (lower); Garrick Palmer 139; Photograph Studio 390 107; Michael Pinder 104; Utte Sanne 128; Patrick Shanahan 30 (lower); Anne Marie Shillito 45; Harriet St Leger 49 (upper); Georgina Taylor 89 (lower); Sarah Tomlin 85; Malcolm Vaugan 97; Carlo Verda 47; Jeanne Werge-Hartley 7, 36, 40 (lower), 43 (upper and lower), 46, 93, 101, 143.

Photograph previous page: *Firebird brooch based on the ballet by Stravinsky.* Jeanne Werge-Hartley, 1998.

Typefaces used: Plantin (main text and headings) and ITC Franklin Gothic (boxes).

Typeset and designed by
D & N Publishing
Baydon, Marlborough, Wiltshire.

Printed and bound in Singapore by Craft Print International Ltd.

CONTENTS

INTRODUCTION

Jewellery should aspire to be an art, as considered in its use of shape and form as painting, as thoughtful in its form as sculpture and as functional in its design as engineering, every aspect combining in a result which enhances and adorns the human body. It should evolve through a creative process in which the maker's perception of form, his experience of techniques, and his understanding of materials enable him to develop intuitive relationships of shape, colour, pattern and texture, which emerges as an individual solution existing in its totality of design on the wearer.

Jeanne Werge-Hartley, 1978

In a very basic sense, a piece of jewellery is an object that relates in scale and function to the human body. Jewellery has been made in every culture of the world for as long as there are records of human history. There appears to be a universal human need to decorate and adorn the human body and for these objects to be special to the people who wear them. Often it is the jewellery that tells archaeologists the most about ancient cultures. The fusing of technology, aesthetics and symbolism, and the fact that since these objects were treasured, they survived, means that they are immensely valuable as a source of information. Jewellery has been made for so many different reasons, for spiritual and symbolic reasons, as amulets and talismans, for sentimental reasons as pledges and keepsakes and to declare status and wealth. During this century there has been a further development in the making of jewellery (alongside other crafts) for it to be a vehicle for personal expression. As a discipline, jewellery attracts many more creative individuals than ever before. When my mother, Jeanne Werge-Hartley took the final exam of the National Design Diploma at Leeds College of Art in 1952 she was one of only three that year, in this country, to specialize in jewellery. Today more that twenty-five colleges and universities run jewellery programmes to degree or higher diploma level and in addition there are a number of postgraduate courses including the Royal College of Art. As a craft, jewellery is moving from being a mostly skills-based discipline to being a far more intellectual, critically aware medium.

To begin to understand any subject it helps to be aware of its history and its cultural significance. It is a very important part of the learning process to look at what was made in the past and to see what contemporary makers are producing today, to understand that makers work in the context of what has gone before and what is happening now, not in isolation. Learning any art-related subject also involves developing your perception of line, form, colour and texture, and the more you look and draw, the better. The ability to draw is something everyone is capable of doing to a reasonably competent level with practice. The aim should be to heighten your visual awareness by actively looking and appreciating the world around you, helping you to develop original and personal ideas. Finally the technical skills of making, and knowledge of the materials you are using are, of course, extremely important. Poor or clumsy craftsmanship can ruin a good idea, although even excellent craftsmanship cannot compensate for a weak design.

The making of a piece of jewellery should look effortless. The blood and sweat should not be apparent in the finished object. A virtuoso piece showing high levels of technical knowledge but poor design is purely craft skill, one can admire it for the difficulty in creating it, but it is not art. The idea, the concept is the most important thing, the craft skills are only a vehicle to translate those ideas into three dimensions.

A comparison could be made with ballet and gymnastics, the latter being about difficulty and technique with only some marks given for artistic expression. The former is an expressive art form that values dancers' abilities to use their bodies apparently effortlessly – dancers should not be seen to sweat or strain! You know that skill and hard work have gone into the preparation but they are not evident in the performance.

As a teacher I can best communicate my way of doing things, a culmination of the teaching I received and my subsequent experience as a maker. My way is not the only one – you will find there are many different techniques (almost as many as there are jewellers) and much disagreement on how to set about things. It is really important to get to know the materials you are working with so that you can anticipate cause and effect. No matter how much you are told how to do something, nothing beats the experience of handling the materials and making mistakes. If anyone tells you pedantically that you should or shouldn't do something then ask why, and if they can't answer satisfactorily, try it anyway; you may then find out that there is a good reason for doing something in a particular way but at least you will find out! However, apart from differing approaches to the work in hand, individual preferences or availability of tools and equipment play a big part in your decision-making. Never be afraid to experiment, try to work out for yourself the best way to tackle a technical problem, and don't just take advice on blind trust. Sometimes the mistakes you make can add to the piece – that is, if you literally go back to the drawing board, more creative solutions may emerge. It is very unusual for a mistake to be so disastrous that there is nothing that can be done to rescue it.

So many jewellery techniques have been developed throughout so many different cultures and periods of history that it would be impossible to know, understand and be proficient in all of them. Most studio jewellers have acquired a particular range of skills that are relevant to their ideas and interests. In addition there are also many companies offering specialist skills that can be used for techniques such as casting, plating, photo etching and engraving so that your ideas can stretch beyond the limits of your own workshop. This book aims to introduce the basic tools, materials and skills of making as well as some thoughts on how to develop your own ideas. Once you have learnt the basic processes you can go on adding to your knowledge for the rest of your life, acquiring new skills, because that is where your ideas have led you.

The pieces of jewellery chosen to illustrate this book are by professional studio jewellers or students, and have all been chosen hopefully to inspire and encourage you. Remember that they, too, all had to start at the beginning once.

Peacock necklace. Silver and crysophrase. Jeanne Werge-Hartley, 1952.

1 STUDIO JEWELLERY IN BRITAIN

This chapter is a brief survey of the development of studio jewellery in Britain. It looks at the way jewellers are educated, the groups of people and associations who have helped to foster and encourage studio jewellery and finally some of the changes in ideas that have informed current thinking.

The term studio jewellery refers to work that has been produced by an individual usually working alone or with a small number of assistants. The maker has total control over the process from idea to end result giving the work a strong personal identity. This way of working is a relatively recent development and is the result of the many changes both in society as a whole, in the way jewellers are educated, and in the way jewellery is seen and worn. This chapter is a very general survey of some of the people, organizations, events and shifts in attitude that have changed the way jewellery is thought about and made. Reading through magazine articles, exhibition catalogues and conference papers it is extraordinary just how many people are involved and how much jewellery has been made, shown and discussed in the twentieth century.

During the Renaissance it was normal practice for an artist to learn the art of goldsmithing alongside painting and sculpture. Cellini's *Treatise on Goldsmithing* is still in print and very interesting to read. However, apart from a few exceptions, until the twentieth century jewellers were artisans who worked anonymously and who were trained through workshop-based apprenticeship systems. As industrialization increased and with it the pressure to make things quicker and cheaper, the growing jewellery manufacturing trade got around the problem of mass producing objects that involved a lot of hand skills, by splitting up the processes, so that even today a trade jeweller trained through an apprentice will be a diamond mounter (the person who does the fine metalwork 'engineering' of a piece) or a setter (setting the stones) or a polisher or an engraver and rarely will they work outside their specialist field. This results in a very high level of skill and a faster speed of production but loses all individuality in the work. The social and technological changes in the twentieth century have provided a climate in which creativity and individuality have become valued, it has meant that many more people than ever before, particularly women, have had the time to think beyond the inevitable drudgery of basic survival and have been able to devote time to creative activities. The interest in craft objects and the concern for quality and individuality have led to a huge growth in the number of people making jewellery, both at amateur and professional level, and with the increase in specialist retail outlets such as galleries and selling exhibitions like Dazzle at the Festival Hall, there are now greater opportunities for the general public to see and buy work.

In studying the development of studio jewellery it is helpful to look at the way design education has changed over the last two hundred years. In the early part of the nineteenth century industrialization had badly affected the quality of design in this country. Henry Cole, amongst others, had

OPPOSITE PAGE: Chain necklace. Textured platinum and fine gold, fused inner surface. Jacqueline Mina, 2000.

seen the problems and tried hard to promote good design, setting up the first art and design schools. However, manufacturers could not be persuaded to see the value of employing designers and the Crystal Palace exhibition in 1851 was heavily criticized for being cluttered with overdecorated pieces where the decoration seemed totally unrelated to the forms of the objects. The Arts and Crafts movement prompted by Ruskin and led by William Morris reacted against the poor quality of design evident in manufactured goods. The idea that there was an honesty in hand-made objects and that even in this time of mass production there was value in working materials by hand led to the setting up of trade schools to teach furniture-making, textiles and silversmithing. The National Art Training school (later to become the Royal College of Art) set up a series of courses in 1905 that included metalwork, the beginnings of the department of silversmithing and jewellery. During the early part of the twentieth century, art schools were mainly small local independent institutions and those jewellery departments that existed were mostly part-time. A national qualification was introduced between the First and Second World Wars called the National Diploma in Design that consisted of two years of general art education to intermediate level followed by two years of specialization leading to the NDD. The Second World War inevitably had a serious effect on the art schools although many struggled on. The Royal College of Art moved up to Ambleside in 1940 and set up very basic workshops with the minimum of tools in two adjoining hotels, not returning to London until 1945. After the Second World War, the government heavily subsidized night-school courses in all subjects in an effort to encourage people whose education had been interrupted or curtailed. This explosion in amateur activity had initially a positive effect on the number of

people becoming interested and involved in the crafts, but eventually a negative effect on the overall perception of the word 'craft' as it became synonymous with poorly made, homespun or crude objects.

The way design students should be educated had been argued over and debated since the first art colleges were set up, the arguments basically polarizing between those who felt that design students should have a broad art-based education and those who felt the training should be about focusing on what industry needed. Should students be taught what they needed to know or should their education facilitate their own process of discovery? This argument still rumbles on today in all areas of education. The 1960s saw the change from the old National Diploma in Design to the Diploma of Art and Design and finally to the introduction of the foundation year to be followed by a three-year degree. This had an enormous effect on studio jewellery. The intellectual content of the courses developed and students were questioning not just how to make jewellery but why. Working alongside painters and sculptors and studying history of art all helped to stimulate new ideas and concepts. The 1960s was a great time for experimentation and the jewellery course at Hornsea College of Art (later to become Middlesex Polytechnic) run by Gerda Flockinger was producing exciting and innovative work. The Central School of Art and Design started a new course in 1965 in the workshops vacated by the trade apprentices who were moved to the John Cass College in Whitechapel. This new course was to go on to produce many inventive and influential jewellers.

During the 1970s some of the colleges broadened their courses to enable more erosion of the boundaries between different craft disciplines. Brighton Polytechnic's Wood, Metal, Ceramics and Plastics course was one of these focusing on ideas rather than the learning of skills. There was a general movement to reject the teaching of skills during the 70s and 80s as they were perceived to be restrictive and inhibiting which indeed they can be if taught in a rigid and inflexible way. Over the last thirty years many of the courses have developed particular characteristics, some emphasizing skills and precious metals and others with more emphasis on ideas and creativity; some actively preparing students to work in the jewellery manufacturing industries as designers, others focusing more on the independent studio jeweller approach. This variety helps to stimulate many divergent and individual approaches to designing and making and it is to be hoped that with the current threat of a national curriculum for higher education, this broad choice for future students will not be lost.

The role of the art societies in the development of studio jewellery has also been an important one. The Art Workers Guild was formed in 1884 and still exists today at Number 6, Queens Square in London where the main meeting hall has all the members' names painted round the room in gold lettering. The guild, founded by five architects, Horsley, Lethaby, Newton, Macartney and Prior, was intended as an opportunity for architects, artists and crafts people to come together to discuss their work and to promote education in all the visual arts and crafts. Out of this group there came the Arts and Crafts Exhibition Society with Walter Crane as its first president. Its aim, as its name suggests, was to exhibit and promote the work of its members. They held their first exhibition in

'Morning Dew'. Tied nylon with PVC and beads. Norah Fok, 1990.

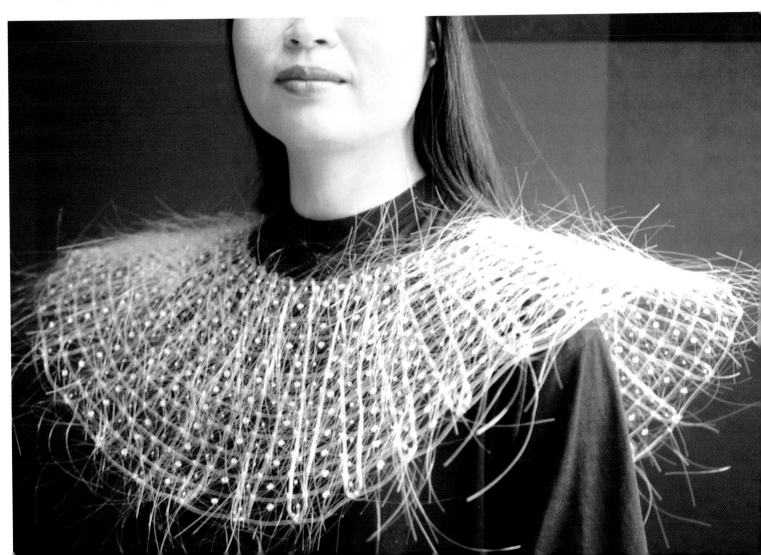

1888. The jewellery that was made at this time was sometimes quite simple but had a liveliness and vitality but was very different from the manufactured objects. The society continued to exhibit and support the work of its members. In response to the change in perception of the word craft during the 1950s and 1960s, the Arts and Crafts Exhibition Society, during the process of amalgamating with the Cambridge Society of Arts and Crafts, changed its name to the Society of Designer Craftsmen that is still the largest society of professional makers in this country.

In the early 1960s the Design Council supported by the government was, under Sir Paul Riley, given the brief to promote contemporary jewellery and did so through a series of exhibitions called 'Shopping in Britain' that ran successfully from the Design Council exhibition space in the Haymarket. The Minister for the Arts, Lord Eccles supported and encouraged the setting up in 1971 of the Crafts Advisory Committee (later to become The Crafts Council) by the Design Council to administer the government grant to the crafts. Under its first director Victor Margrie it established an exhibition space and an index of professional makers in Waterloo Place and remained there until the need for more space necessitated the move to its present Islington home. In addition to its own exhibitions it also supported the British Crafts Centre in Covent Garden that later moved to Percy Street and became Contemporary Applied Arts, and in the 1980s it started the Chelsea Craft Fair that aims to show the newest and best contemporary work. The Crafts Council is also responsible for supporting individual craftsmen through its system of grants and, in addition, publishes books and the magazine *Crafts*.

Another major supporter of studio jewellery has been the Goldsmiths Company, first given its royal charter in 1327. It has been collecting silverware since 1350 but did not start collecting jewellery until the 1960s with Graham Hughes as an enthusiastic promoter of contemporary jewellery. The Goldsmiths Company is one of the oldest of the London trade guilds and is still very much involved in supporting and promoting the work of contemporary jewellers and silversmiths both in the manufacturing trade and the studio craft area. In 1961 Graham Hughes organized the International Exhibition of Modern Jewellery (1890–1961) the first of its kind in which the work of jewellers such as Andrew Grima, David Thomas, John Donald, Friedrich Becker, Gillian Packard and Louis Osman were seen for the first time by a wider audience. Then in 1975 the first of the 'Loot' exhibitions was held – these were open entry and anyone could submit work to be selected. They were held over seven years until 1981 when the newly formed Department of Design and Technology replaced them with the Goldsmiths Fair that continues to run annually.

Inevitably one of the problems of working as a studio jeweller is that of isolation, and in order to promote and exhibit their work other smaller independent groups have formed. Out of an original discussion that took place between seven jeweller members of the Society of Designer Craftsmen, the Designer Jewellers Group began with sixteen members at the London Fashion Week in 1976 with Gillian Packard as its first chairman. The main aim of the group was to promote the work of the members through exhibitions and the main criterion for membership of the group was to have a strong individual style. The group exhibited together at the Design Centre, the Goldsmiths Fair and at the Earls Court Trade Fair and at numerous other venues over the next few years. In 1984 the first DJG exhibition at the Barbican Centre was held and this has now become an annual event. Of the original sixteen only Jeanne Werge-Hartley and Stephen Maer are still with the group that has expanded to the present thirty members. Over the years the membership has changed but the original aims and criteria for membership have remained constant. Other groups have also formed to work together and share the costs of workshop space. Studio 4011/2, the Clerkenwell and the Oxo Tower workshops are in London but other areas of the country have also formed similar groups.

Until 1996 there had not been a single association representing the need of all studio jewellers in Britain. In the USA, the Society of North American Goldsmiths began in the autumn of 1968 and currently has a membership of around 2,500. SNAG also publish the journal *Metalsmith* and hold conferences to give studio jewellers the opportunity to discuss what they do and why.

However, in 1996 a conference 'The Jewellers' Exchange' was organized by Norman Cherry at the University of Northumbria prompted by discussions initiated by Dee Dine at the Darlington Arts Centre. From this conference came the Association of Contemporary Jewellery, an inclusive organization for anyone involved in jewellery whether as makers, teachers, collectors or enthusiasts. It held its first conference in Edinburgh in 1998 that coincided with an exciting international exhibition called 'Jewellery Moves'. It followed this with another very successful conference called 'A Sense of Wonder' held in Birmingham in 2000 that attracted many European and American delegates. The ACJ also produces a quarterly newsletter and is building strong links with other associations such as SNAG.

There have also been various competitions that have given opportunities to either practising studio jewellers or to students on full-time courses. The Royal Society of Arts Bursary and in the 1980s the Platinum Competition sponsored by Ayrton Metals, gave students the chance to experience working in a material that would normally be outside most student budgets. By freeing them from the constraints of cost, they were able to do some interesting and experimental work. For professionals there is the Diamonds International Competition and the Goldsmiths Competition in partnership with the Crafts Council. A recent development has been the Jerwood Prize that is awarded to a different craft each year and has twice been awarded for jewellery with the year 2000 award going to Jacqueline Mina.

It is in the area of ideas that studio jewellery has changed radically during the twentieth century and the greater part of that change has occurred in the last thirty years. In the first half of the twentieth century many fine artists were interested in the possibilities of jewellery, amongst them Picasso, Braque and Dali all experimented with designing jewellery. Dali in particular was concerned that the cost of the materials was obscuring the more important value of the quality of the idea and its execution. Other fine artists like Geo and Arnaldo Pomadoro, Tanguy, Dubuffet, Giacometti, Jean Arp and Alexander Calder all produced jewellery intended to overcome this overvaluing of the materials, to give prominence to the idea, the concept. During the 1930s and 1940s, interest in studio jewellery amongst artists in America was strong and, rejecting the 'how many diamonds can you get to the square inch?' school, they made jewellery for each other and for their social group. Alexander Calder, in particular, made and exhibited jewellery that for a time became more important to him than his sculpture. In Britain the Second World War had seen the jewellery trade come to a virtual standstill with the shortage of materials and workshops taken over for essential war work. The introduction of purchase tax that at one point stood at 125 per cent completely stifled the possibility of the trade introducing any new ideas and those manufacturers that survived were reliant on traditional designs. The dominance of 9kt gold in the mass production market is a direct

'The Future is at our Fingertips'. Finger Extensions. Knitted pigmented nylon. Norah Fok, 1999.

result of the high rates of tax. It was the 1950s before studio jewellery really started again to make some impact with Gerda Flockinger, who originally trained as a painter, as a foremost figure.

Jewellery designs of the 1950s and early 1960s was strongly influenced by the work of Scandinavian jeweller and silversmith George Jensen. The clean uncluttered lines and shapes of Scandinavian design are still considered by many of the general public as modern design. In contrast much of the jewellery of the 1960s was rich in surface and texture. Work by Andrew Grima, John Donald and Gillian Packard used decoration and surfaces that on a visual level at least had links with some of the sculpture of the time. The work was in precious metals often using naturally occurring crystals sometimes combined with cut stones. By the late 1960s the courses at Hornsea and Central had jewellers emerging who were

producing individual and very different work – for example, Charlotte De Syllas and David Poston from Hornsea and Wendy Ramshaw (originally trained in fabric design and illustration at Newcastle) from Central where she spent a year developing her lathe-turned work.

The mid-1960s saw Dutch jewellers Emmy Van Leersum and Gils Bakker exhibiting aluminium collars and cuffs that were a radical new departure. Rejecting precious materials they worked in industrial materials and helped to influence a new generation of jewellers just emerging from British art schools. The West German jewellers were another strong influence. Germany's rich tradition of jewellery flourished after 1945 and Hermann Junger as a jeweller and Professor of Goldsmithing at the Academy of Fine Arts in Munich has, through his teaching and his own work, encouraged very high levels of craftsmanship as well as new and exciting ideas. Friedrich Becker with the development of kinetic jewellery and Reinhold Reiling the Professor of Jewellery at the Art School at Pforzheim have also been a major influence. By the early 1970s non-precious jewellery was beginning to be shown in London; in 1971, for instance, the Electrum Gallery displayed work in acrylic by three German jewellers and an Austrian. Amongst those graduating from college at this time were Caroline Broadhead, Susanna Heron, Julia Manheim, Eric Spiller and Nuala Jamison. Influenced by work coming out of Holland and West Germany, 'The New Jewellery' Movement as it came to be known, rejected traditional precious metals and stones as they were loaded with all the negative elitist connotations of wealth and status. They worked in alternative materials, plastics, steel, aluminium, rubber. They tried to make the work more easily accessible by producing multiples. The fresh and exciting work being produced at this time went on to influence the European jewellers in return. In 1981 an exhibition at the British Craft Centre called 'Jewellery Redefined' brought together many of the people and ideas in a major exhibition where precious materials were almost completely absent. The use of non-precious materials dominated studio jewellery for the next decade enthusiastically supported by Ralph Turner at the Crafts Council. Consequently very little work in precious metal was shown at Waterloo Place. Of course many jewellers continued to work in precious metal, particularly Wendy Ramshaw, Jacqueline Mina and Kevin Coates and recently many of those who rejected it have now come back to working with it once again. Possibly because of that period of rejection, precious metals seem to occupy a different place – that is, not as separate and distinct from the 'alternative' materials but as just some of the many possible materials available to be used.

In the last twenty years jewellery has continued to develop and change. Increasing opportunities to see contemporary jewellery in galleries, exhibitions and books, better communication enabling a faster exchange of ideas and influence have all helped to make contemporary jewellery an incredibly diverse and exciting area. Contemporary jewellers approach their work from many different directions and look to various source materials and influences. Some work through the philosophical questioning of what they are doing – that is, why adorn the body? why make these objects? why wear these objects? Some work from the materials and their unique properties and qualities, expanding their understanding of material and process. Some work instinctively with shape and form within a narrow range of materials. Some mix materials and choose to work in whatever is appropriate to their current ideas. Some work from their environment and natural form, some from historical artifacts or from painting or sculpture. Ultimately they are all individuals bringing their own characters, experiences and interests to bear on a discipline that has had its parameters blown wide open. The 'Jewellery Moves' exhibition at the Edinburgh Museum in 1998 showed just how divergent some of the ideas can be, ranging from the decorative to the conceptual, from social comment to theatre. As in all art forms there are those who push out the boundaries, who experiment and provoke dissent. Often for the beginner the latest most experimental work will not fit with their expectations of what jewellery should be, the work may seem unwearable and outlandish to the uninitiated, but it is the makers who are pushing and stretching ideas who take the whole of the art form forward and influence all of us working within the discipline. Without them we would not have seen the explosion of creative activity over the last part of the twentieth century.

2 BASIC TOOLS AND EQUIPMENT

OPPOSITE PAGE:
Basic tool kit.

1. *French blow torch*
2. *Ring mandrel*
3. *Round-nosed pliers*
4. *Snipe pliers*
5. *Flat pliers*
6. *Bench peg*
7. *Heat-resistant blocks*
8. *Bob drill*
9. *Centre punch*
10. *Dividers*
11. *Brass tweezers*
12. *Steel tweezers*
13. *Snips*
14. *Saw frame*
15. *Needle files*
16. *Paintbrush*
17. *Ruler*
18. *Scribe*
19. *Jobbing hammer*
20. *Ball pein hammer*
21. *Rawhide mallet*

The range and variety of tools available for a jeweller to use is extraordinary and initially rather bewildering. The jewellery industry is much larger than many people realize and there is much support from specialized tool manufacturers and suppliers. New tools are being developed all the time and the catalogues produced by the tool manufacturers are inspiring even if they do make you feel like a child in a sweet shop. All of the tool companies produce well-illustrated catalogues and will send tools by mail order. There are some wonderful, highly specialized tools ranging from a small unit that stamps out different-sized circles to highly sophisticated computer software that allows you to design a piece of jewellery on the screen. (The computer then downloads the image to another piece of equipment that creates a three-dimensional model in wax for casting.) However, many of these tools are largely about making basic processes simpler and quicker and therefore to make production more cost effective rather than supplying you with things that you cannot do without. Initially the basic range of tools described in this chapter will enable the beginner to start and gradually as your ideas develop and your skills grow, you can add more tools as necessary. It is often worth while looking at tool stalls in markets as sometimes they have cheap versions of scribes, files and pliers. The quality is not very good but it is a start and will do until you can afford to get better ones. Well-made tools are expensive but will last much longer if looked after properly.

THE WORKBENCH

It is very important to have an organized area to work in. This need not take up a large amount of space but you need to have a stable and solid workbench to work on. The traditional bench with a curve cut out and a tray or skin to catch the lemel (waste metal) is ideal but not essential. Because making jewellery often involves sitting for quite long periods of time in one position it is important to have your bench at the right height. Make sure that it is high enough so that you can sit with your back straight and also that your chair supports your back properly.

Light is also really important. If possible work near a window to give you maximum natural light without being in direct

Workbench.

sunlight. An anglepoise lamp with a daylight bulb is vital for days when there is not enough natural light. Warmth is also essential. It is difficult to sit still while working on delicate pieces if you are cold and, because you are not moving around, you tend to feel the cold more quickly.

ORGANIZING YOUR TOOLS

It is very helpful to organize your tools so that they are close to hand when you need them. Jam jars can be used as containers – for example, needle files can be put in one, tweezers and pliers in another. Alternatively you could use the magnetic strips that are available for storing kitchen knives. However you organize them try to get into the habit of putting tools back when you have used them so that you always know where to find them again.

THE BASIC KIT

This list includes all the basic tools that you need to start with and to complete the projects included in this book.

A Scribe

A scribe is a piece of steel that comes to a sharp point used for marking out metal.

150mm Steel Ruler

A small steel ruler for measuring and for marking out the metal.

Various hammers; (left to right) jobbing hammer for use with punches, a 4oz ball pein hammer for working directly onto the surface of metal and a rawhide mallet for working metal without damaging the surface.

Small Pair of Dividers

Dividers are used for transferring measurements and for marking out the metal.

Centre Punch

A centre punch is a steel punch with a point for locating the position to drill a hole.

Pliers

The three pairs of pliers that are necessary are flat, snipe and round-ended. Used for bending and shaping the metal, pliers become virtual extensions to your fingers.

7-inch Straight Shears

Shears are for cutting solder and small pieces of metal.

Saw Frame

A saw frame for cutting metal, a wooden handle and metal frame with two clamps for holding a saw blade and sometimes another clamp to enable the saw frame to be adjusted to take a shorter length of broken saw blade.

A Bench Peg

A bench peg is a wedge-shaped piece of wood that is either screwed or clamped to the workbench to enable you to saw and file metal unimpeded and in a comfortable position.

Tweezers

One pair of fine pointed steel tweezers and a pair of brass tweezers or plastic (for pickling).

Fine Paintbrush (Cheap)

For painting the metal with flux or FM solution and for picking up small pieces of solder.

Files

There is more information about files later in this chapter but start with a basic set of needle files. These are sold as a set that usually consists of six different cross sections (usually round, half round, pillar, square, three square and crossing). Two hand files, a flat and a half round 150mm grade 2 are also useful.

Bob Drill

A bob drill consists of a chuck just below a brass counterweight on a steel rod drilled at the top with a wooden crossbar attached by string through the hole in the steel rod. This is a very ancient design of drill but very effective. Using it takes a little practice but like playing with a yo-yo once you have learnt it, it is easy. Put a drill into the chuck leaving only the thickness of the metal to be drilled showing (fine drills are very brittle and expensive – the more drill length exposed the more the drill will flex and the more likely it is to break). Make sure the strings are running straight and the crossbar is horizontal. Hold the top of the rod and spin the bar so that the string winds itself around the rod in a spiral. Place the fingers of one hand on the crossbar either side of the rod and use your thumb to stop the string unwinding until you are ready. Place the point of the drill onto the centre-punched mark and give a gentle push down. You are only providing momentum, the counterweight will do the rest. With practice it is possible to speed up and slow down and control what you are doing far better than with an electric drill.

Rawhide Mallet

A rawhide mallet is made, as the name suggests, of animal hide. This mallet is essential as it allows you to directly hit and shape metal without damaging the surface.

Metal Hammers

A 4oz ball pein hammer for working directly onto the surface of the metal.

A small jobbing hammer to use with punches.

Ring Mandrel

A ring mandrel (sometimes called a triblet) is a tapered steel cone for making rings circular.

Torches for Annealing and Soldering

There are several different torches that can be used for soldering. Many jewellers, the author included, use a French blowtorch or mouth blow-torch. Some are designed to work using natural gas and some with propane, combined with air that is introduced into the flame by blowing down a tube held in your mouth. It takes some practice and although at first you might find the breath control needed difficult it is an excellent method of heating the metal when working small-scale and can be run either straight off the main supply via a bayonet fitting or from a camping gas bottle with an adaptor on top. There are also various small hand torches on the market that run on Butane or lighter fuel which are very portable and easy to use although they are only useful for very small work. In a workshop a Sievert torch is generally used for larger-scale pieces; these run on either natural gas or propane with a compressor supplying the air. There are other types of torch but these are the ones you are most likely to use.

Heat-Resistant Blocks for Soldering

When annealing or soldering you need a heat-resistant area to work in. Soldering sheets and blocks are used to build up a small area in which you can confine the heat. The minimum needed is two 300mm square soldering sheets and a soldering block. Two

French blowtorch.

Further tools.

1 *Small square mandrel*
2 *Small round mandrel*
3 *Large square mandrel*
4 *Parallel pliers*
5 *Half-round pliers*
6 *Three square scraper*
7 *Curved steel burnisher*
8 *Straight steel burnisher*
9 *Agate burnisher*
10 *Brass setting pusher*
11 *Steel block*
12 *Riffler files*
13 *Square*
14 *Pin vice*
15 *Hand vice*
16 *Mini anvil*
17 *Small bench vice*
18 *Half-round hand file*
19 *Pillar hand file*
20 *Pillar file with handle*
21 *Small hammer with interchangeable heads*
22 *Riveting hammer*

pieces of wood screwed together at right angles to support the soldering sheets make an effective small hearth. There are some alternatives to the basic soldering blocks – honeycomb ceramic soldering boards are very useful as are ceramic fire bricks. Charcoal blocks are excellent although you must remember to quench them in water after using or your expensive block of charcoal will be a small pile of ash next time you look. Other useful materials for soldering are squares of steel mesh or a soldering wig.

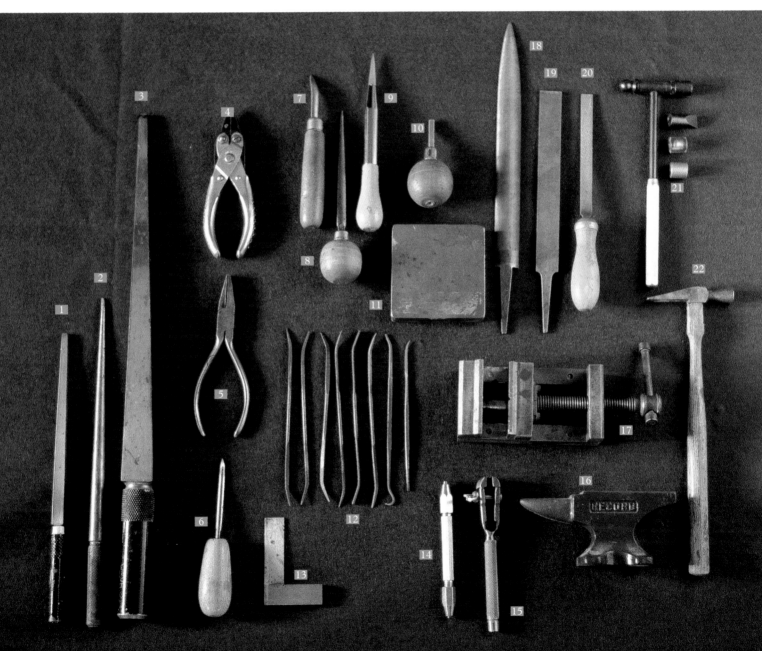

FURTHER USEFUL TOOLS

In addition to the basic kit, the following are some of the tools you will also find in most jewellers' workshops. It is not necessary to buy them straightaway, but as you find you need them. Joining a part-time class is a good idea to begin with as it will give you access to larger tools that you may not be able to buy immediately, as well as the chance to benefit from the skills of the person teaching the class. In some areas it is possible to rent bench space per day which is another way of having access to tools like rolling mills and polishing motors.

Three Square Scraper

A triangular hand tool with three sharp edges, it is useful for removing excess solder and firestain particularly from the inside of rings.

Parallel Pliers

As the name suggests, pliers that open and close with the jaws parallel.

Half-Round Pliers

These have one side curved and one side flat and are useful for curving metal.

Setting Pusher

A short length of round or square section steel or brass rod about 4mm diameter with a round wooden handle for pushing the metal over a stone for setting. A brass pusher is preferable as brass is softer and will mark your work less if you slip.

Burnishers

Smoothly shaped steel or agate tools with wooden handles. They are used to smooth the surface of the metal and are a method of polishing that was in use long before the abrasive methods of today.

Square

A steel right angle for marking out metal and checking angles when you are filing.

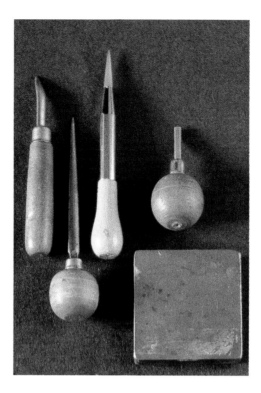

Burnishing tools.

Pin Vice

A small chuck on a handle useful for holding wires or tools.

Hand Vice

A small vice on a handle useful for holding small pieces for filing.

Small Engineers Bench Vice

A small vice (jaws about 60mm across).

Engineer Files

These come in three grades smooth, 2 cut and bastard, and range from 150mm to 300mm long.

Hand Files

These come in various grades dependent on the shape ranging from 00 (fine) to 6 (coarse) and are 150mm to 200mm long. Engineer and hand files come without handles. Wooden handles can be bought separately and fitted by heating the tong of the file and then pushing the wooden handle onto the heated spike.

Needle Files and Escapement Files

These come in a range of grades, profiles and lengths, the usual is 140mm long cut 2. They can be bought individually or in sets.

Riffler Files

These have curved and shaped ends, very useful for getting into awkward places.

Seconds Files

Round or square section, these are very small (75mm long), very fine files.

Hammers and Mallets

A riveting hammer. A company in USA make a small hammer with interchangeable heads (steel ball, cross and flat, brass flat, acrylic flat) that is very good value.

Steel Block

A machined steel block about 75mm square for levelling and checking that pieces are flat.

Baby Anvil (120mm long)

This is used for small-scale forging.

Mandrels (sometimes called triblets)

These are tapered steel cones in different sizes. The tapers range from 25mm–8mm

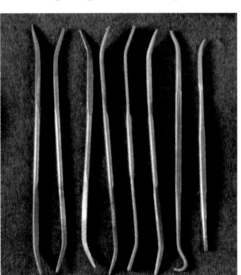

FAR LEFT: *Mandrels (triblets).*
LEFT: *Riffler files.*
BELOW: *Drawplates and draw tongs.*

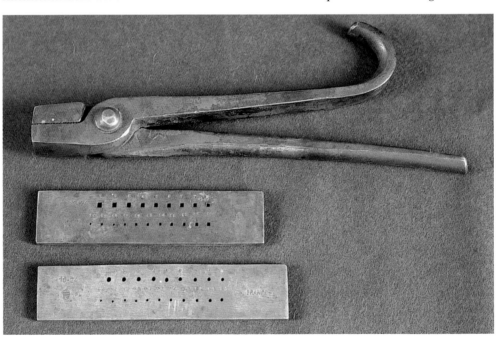

for rings – smaller ones (12mm–3mm) for settings and links and larger (90mm–50mm) for bangles. Other shapes are made too including triangular, oval, square, even hexagonal and pear-shaped.

Swage Block
A steel block with curves machined into it for shaping pieces of metal.

Doming Block and Doming Punches
The former comes in steel or brass and the latter in steel or wood.

Pendant Drill
An electric motor suspended from a bracket or a hook in the ceiling that drives a flexible drive shaft with a chuck at the end of it. They are usually controlled by a foot pedal that allows you to vary the speed of the shaft. The pendant drill can be used for drilling, cleaning up and polishing, grinding, texturing and carving.

Polishing Machines
These are important if you want to achieve a high polish on your work and small ones are made that are suitable for a small workshop. It is sensible to buy one with built-in extraction so that you do not cover your workshop (and yourself) with a thin film of rouge. Even with extraction it is best to wear a dust mask when polishing.

Draw Plates
These are steel plates with holes tapering in size for drawing wire down (reducing the thickness or changing the

section). They are made for every different-shaped wire imaginable – however, most jewellers have at least two drawplates for round and square wire.

Draw Tongs
Heavy steel tongs with one curved handle for pulling wire through drawplates. For a workshop at home a pair of parallel pliers will do.

Draw Bench
This enables heavier wire to be pulled down easily by using a winding system to increase the leverage you can exert. It is unlikely that you would use one enough to justify the expense of buying one but most well-equipped workshops where jewellery is taught will have one.

Rolling Mill
This is like a small, very accurate mangle and is used for rolling metal thinner. It has two steel rollers and can be adjusted to increase or decrease the gap between them by means of a screw. Mills can either be fitted to the end of a workbench or mounted on a stand. Ideally the stand should be bolted to the floor; however, if this is not practical it can be bolted to a flat piece of

Forming and shaping tools.

1. *Boxwood doming punches*
2. *Steel doming punches*
3. *Swage block*
4. *Doming block*
5. *Small swage block*
6. *Small doming block*

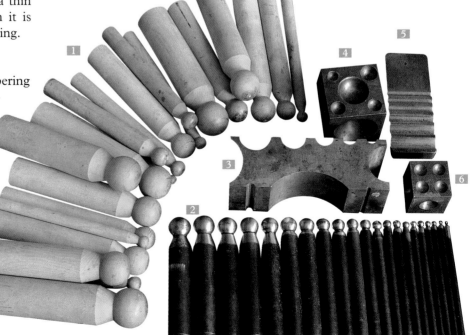
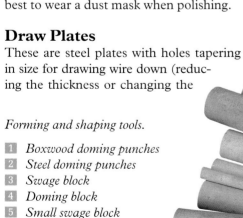

FAR RIGHT: Rolling mill.

wood sufficiently large to enable you to stand on it while using the rolling mill to keep it in place. Some rollers include slots for square, round wire and half round. Patterned rollers are also made to produce decorative finishes but this would only be worth the expense for a commercial business. Roller printing is a technique more suited to the individual maker (*see* Chapter 5).

Model-Maker's Lathe

This can be very useful and some models come with a range of attachments for milling and sawing. It is also useful to make sure that the model you choose can be used for free turning, using hand tools and a

Lathe with milling attachment.

rest, as well as precision turning with fixed tools clamped in a tool post. Free turning is less restrictive than precision turning but can only be done with softer materials like wood, plastic, and softer metals such as silver, brass and copper.

Kiln

If you are interested in using particular materials such as 1715 hardenable silver, precious metal clay or you would like eventually to incorporate porcelain or enamels into your work then a kiln is necessary. Suitable kilns are made for enamelling but it is important to get one with a pyrometer so the temperature can be gauged accurately. Ceramic test kilns are not suitable for enamelling and 1715 silver as they usually have safety cut-out mechanisms on the door that makes keeping the temperature constant very difficult if the door is frequently opened and shut.

CONSUMABLES

Piercing Saw Blades

Finest 8/0 7/0 6/0 5/0 4/0 3/0 2/0 1/0 0 1 2 3 4 5 6 *coarsest*.

Piercing saw blades range from the finest 8/0, for very intricate designs in gold where it is important to lose as little metal as possible, to 6 which is extremely coarse. The thickness of the blade depends on the thickness of the metal you intend to cut and the intricacy of the shape. As a general rule, choose a saw blade so that there are three teeth to the thickness of the metal you are intending to saw. 3/0 is a fairly general purpose size.

Pickling Solutions

There are three alternatives.

Sulphuric Acid

Sulphuric acid can be used as a pickle at a dilution of about 10:1. Make sure you keep it in an acid-proof jar with a stopper and that it is clearly labelled. If diluting acid, *always* add acid to water. Mixing acid with water generates heat and if you pour water into undiluted acid it will react strongly and spit and splash you.

Safety Pickle

Safety pickle comes as a salt that is then mixed with water to a dilution of 80 per cent. This solution works best when kept warm, and in a large workshop a pickle tank keeps the safety pickle at a constant temperature. A slow cooker is another useful way of keeping pickle hot in a small workshop, or a heat-proof dish on a tripod with a nightlight underneath.

Alum

Alum also works very effectively as a pickle. Mix a solution of about a dessertspoonful to ½ litre of water and boil in an old saucepan until the work is clean.

FLUX AND FIRESTAIN INHIBITORS

A flux is used when soldering to enable the solder to flow. It works by inhibiting the formation of oxides around the join and by reducing the surface tension of the solder.

Borax

Borax is the most commonly used flux for silver. It is sold in a cone-shaped lump and is ground down into a paste with water in a borax dish. It is then painted onto the solder and around the join.

FM Solution

It was originally taken from the Goldsmiths Company's special Report No. 15 (published in 1972 by Peter Gainsbury) that was written as a result of a summer seminar run by the Goldsmiths Company at the John Cass in 1971. Amongst other things, the week investigated various solutions that would prevent or at least inhibit the formation of firestain on silver (the team included Jack Stapley and Jeanne Werge-Hartley). The following recipe has been modified over the years from this research. FM solution contains borax and so it can also be used as a flux and is considerably easier to use than traditional borax cones. It also keeps the surface of the metal generally cleaner when heating and although intended specifically for silver it is effective both on gold and on base metals such as copper and brass. To use to maximum effect the metal should be warmed and the solution painted or sprayed on so that it hisses and dries on the surface, forming a complete skin. However, painting the solution on cold every time the metal is heated (for both annealing and soldering) is still very effective. The metal should be matted (any fine abrasive will do) to allow the solution to cover the surface – if the metal is shiny, the surface tension of the solution will not allow an even covering.

Boric acid powder	106.4g
Sodium Acid Phosphate	70g
Sodium Hydroxide (Caustic Soda)	7g
Borax powder	70g
Teepol (or washing-up liquid)	28.4ml
Distilled water	1.5l

METHOD – weigh out the chemicals and dissolve slowly in lukewarm, distilled water stirring constantly. The solution does not seem to deteriorate with age although it is less effective if it gets dirty, so only pour out small amounts for use at a time.

Auflux

Auflux should be used on the solder and around the join when soldering gold.

Heat Protection

There will be times when you need to protect part of your work from heat and there are several pastes or gels made specially for this purpose. These products will also protect some stones from heat and can be used to control decorative surface treatments like reticulation (*see* Chapter 5).

Adhesives

There are basically two sorts of glue that are useful to jewellers, epoxy resins and cyanacrylates. Epoxy resins are two-part glues that when mixed form a very strong bond. There are several different sorts with different lengths of setting time that give both clear and opaque results. Cyanacrylates are the very fast setting 'superglues'. Both types of glue are useful depending on the circumstances. It is always better not to rely totally on glue to hold something together; use it as additional back up or to locate a part before fixing it permanently. Gum Tragacanth is another useful adhesive for locating fine wires before soldering as it burns out. (This glue is often used by enamellers.)

Binding Wire

Iron wire that is supplied in different thicknesses to bind pieces together for soldering. Binding wire should not be put into any pickling solutions as the subsequent chemical reaction will copperplate the work. It is also possible to buy stainless steel binding wire that can be put safely into the pickle. Fine refractory metal wire

can also be used and will not contaminate the pickle.

Drill Bits

Twist drills are made from 0.1mm diameter upwards and can be bought singly or in sets. It is useful to have several of different sizes, 0.9, 1.0, 1.2, 1.5 and 2.0mm would be a start.

Polishing Mops

Polishing mops are made of a variety of different materials resulting in harder or softer mops. Calico or compressed felt are the hardest and swansdown and wool the softest. Felt mops are made in different shapes from cone shapes for polishing inside rings to knife edge for getting into awkward angles. Bristle brushes are very useful and are made in black (coarse) and white (soft). To begin with use a calico mop for Tripoli and a swansdown mop for rouge.

Polishing Threads

Polishing threads are soft cotton threads that are used for polishing – this is known as thrumming. The threads are pinned to the workbench and coated either with Tripoli or rouge (do not use both compounds on the same threads). The threads are then threaded through the work, as many as you can fit and then the threads are held taut and the work moved up and down the threads. The threads will cut quite quickly, particularly with Tripoli, so stop and look frequently.

Mops and Burrs for the Pendant Drill

There is a wide range of metal, stone, rubber and diamond burrs that are produced for use in pendant drills. One very useful tool is a split mandrel into which you can slot a strip of silicon carbide paper that can considerably reduce the time spent cleaning up a piece for polishing. Mops, felts and brushes of all sorts of shapes are also made for the pendant drill for polishing but they are only suitable for very small work.

ABRASIVES
Silicon Carbide
Silicon carbide can be bought from DIY stores in the form of abrasive paper in a range of grades. The most useful of these are between 280 (the coarsest you are likely to need) and 1200 (the finest). There are other abrasive papers available, aluminium oxide, emery, ferrous oxide or crocus paper. It is up to individual taste.

Garriflex
Garriflex is a soft spongy abrasive block that comes in four different grades, very coarse, coarse, medium and fine. The medium and fine are particularly useful for jewellery. It can be cut to shape with a knife to get into specific areas and it is very good for removing firestain.

Pumice
Pumice powder is the abrasive that is commonly used in kitchen and bathroom cleaners. It can be mixed with water to make a paste and used on the surface with the wrong end of a matchstick or a piece of Scotchbrite, or it can be mixed with olive oil and used with a Scotchbrite mop on a polishing motor to give a very fine satin finish.

Scotchbrite
Familiar to most people as green pan scourer for washing up. Scotchbrite comes in different grades of coarseness. You can buy it in flat sheets or made up into mops for the polishing motor.

Water of Ayr Stone
A pale grey naturally occurring fine stone that is produced in sticks of different size and shape. Used with water to remove scratches and other blemishes by gently rubbing on the surface of the work.

Glass-Fibre Sticks
White glass-fibre sticks are used to clean up difficult-to-reach places, very similar to Water of Ayr but not as messy. Use wet or dry. They can be easily filed at the end to customize them to the shape you need.

Glass-Fibre Brush
Fine filaments of glass fibre either in a propelling pencil form or in a bundle bound with string for creating localized satin finishes. That is, if you want a satin finish in a small area leaving other areas shiny then mask the shiny area with masking tape and brush the glass-fibre brush over the area to be satin-finished working in one direction. Polythene or rubber gloves should be worn when using this as the fine pieces of glass fibre can get into your fingers.

Tripoli
Tripoli is a dark yellow abrasive compound used on a polishing mop either on a polishing motor or on a small mop in a flexible drive shaft (pendant drill). It is a fairly coarse compound and will remove metal quite quickly.

Rouge
Rouge is a fine red-colour finishing compound that will produce a high shine when used on polishing mops either on a polishing motor or the pendant drill.

There are many other polishing compounds available as well as Tripoli and rouge. Rouge itself comes in various different forms and it is a matter of personal preference which ones are used. The general principle to be remembered is that you are working from a coarse to a finer compound.

Ammonia
About 1cm of household ammonia in a jam jar with a good squirt of washing-up liquid topped up to half a jarful of hot water makes an excellent solution for removing tripoli and rouge after polishing and for general cleaning and degreasing.

3 MATERIALS

Jewellers have a wide range of materials to work with from precious metals to plastic, from diamonds to paper. All materials, both precious and non-precious, have intrinsic qualities that have an effect on the resulting piece of work. You need to be sensitive to these qualities and to make conscious choices as to which material or combination of materials you are going to choose to work with. Silver, gold and platinum should be used for what they can do as materials and for their suitability for realizing your idea rather than because of some artificial monetary value. However, one of the advantages of non-precious metals in particular is their relative cheapness enabling students to be less inhibited in realizing their ideas even if the intention is to make the piece in precious metal eventually. Many jewellers choose to work entirely in non-precious materials and make the most of the possibilities afforded by their chosen materials, finding imaginative ways of circumventing their limitations. Some jewellers choose to combine precious with non-precious materials which can create problems in the UK if the non-precious material is metal. It is illegal to describe precious metal as such if it is combined in a piece with non-precious metal when being offered for sale. For example: if a piece made with gold and steel is for sale the maker must describe the gold as yellow metal. To describe it as gold in these circumstances is to risk a heavy fine or even imprisonment. If you look at the sheer exuberance with which American jewellers unrestrainedly combine the precious and non-precious, it seems that the UK's hallmarking law may have a restrictive effect on the way we use materials. This chapter will look at some of the materials available to jewellers and ways in which they can be incorporated into jewellery. This is by no means a comprehensive list and it is always fascinating to look at materials produced for other industries and to investigate their potential for jewellery. The materials in this chapter are arranged in alphabetical order.

ALUMINIUM

Aluminium is a lightweight soft metal. It is easy to bend but dirty and difficult to polish. To anneal aluminium, cover with soap and heat until the soap goes black. The quality that is most useful as far as jewellery is concerned is that it can be anodized electrolytically. This means that by passing an electrical current through the metal while it is suspended in an electrolyte (usually a weak acid solution) an anodized layer develops on the surface of the metal. The resulting layer is clear but porous and can be dyed. There are dyes (Sanadol) produced for this purpose but they are very bright rather unsubtle colours. Most other pigments like watercolours or felt pens work well. It is possible to buy pre-anodized aluminium that comes protected from the air by a plastic sheet. Once exposed to the air there is about eight to ten minutes' working time before the surface starts to seal itself. Once colouring is complete, boil the aluminium in water for ten minutes to completely seal it. One way

OPPOSITE PAGE:
Various materials.

to approach the colouring is to colour a sheet as if it is a piece of fabric and then cut out the sections you require. If you need to shape the pieces then protect the surface with masking tape. Then use mechanical fixing to connect the pieces together. Jane Adam is a jeweller best known for her use of aluminium in which she produces rich and colourful patterns that she then cuts into shapes and builds in layers, often riveting parts together.

BRASS

Brass is a yellow-coloured alloy of copper and zinc. There are several different types of brass with varying proportions of copper and zinc, some harder and some softer. One often used by student jewellers because it behaves in a similar way to silver is gilding metal. Brass is a strong alloy for making structures and will take a good polish although it has to be lacquered or sealed with wax or it oxidizes rapidly. Model shops and sometimes DIY stores usually carry an interesting range of different sized tubing, rod and sheet. Brass can be silver soldered and can be annealed by heating to dull red heat and quenching in the same way as silver. Brass can also be satin-finished, textured or patinated using chemicals.

CERAMIC

Clay can be incorporated into jewellery either in bead form or in sections. There are many different types of clay, but one of the most suitable for use in jewellery is porcelain due to its fineness and strength. This may seem unexpected as porcelain is generally thought of as being delicate and fragile, but in the small forms applicable to jewellery it is very strong. Porcelain can be

ABOVE: 'Egyptian Blue' necklace. Silver and anodized aluminium loom-woven and then pleated. Arline Fisch, 1999.

Patinated brass brooches. John McKellar.

Patinated brass box with beads and synthetic hair. Elizabeth Haynes.

formed and shaped with fingers and small tools like lolly sticks and the end of paintbrushes. After it has been left to dry for an hour or two it reaches the 'leather hard' stage where you can refine the shape using a combination of knives, scribes and burnishers (the back of a teaspoon or a small shiny pebble work well as burnishers).

If you are making beads they are easier to drill at this stage. When the piece has totally dried out you can fire the piece in an electric kiln initially to 800°C. As with all ceramic firings the kiln needs to be brought up to heat from cold and then left to cool before the work is taken out. At this temperature the porcelain has not vitrified, which is achieved in the final firing, so it is still fairly fragile although strong enough to be worked on. If the shape needs to be refined further it can be filed with a fine metal file, Water of Ayr stone or smoothed with silicon carbide paper. Any fixing points that you will need to attach the porcelain to the metal, or to attach a finding, need to be drilled (a fine drill bit fixed in a pin vice works well). The porcelain then needs to be fired to 1,260–1,300°C to achieve its final strength and hardness. As with all clay, porcelain shrinks when it is fired so it is usually better to make the metal parts of the piece after the clay is fired if they need to fit accurately. Colour can be added to the clay either in the form of industrially produced stains or raw oxides that are blended into the wet clay before the piece is made. Between the two firings glaze can be applied (the temperature of the second firing will then be dependent on the glaze) and further decoration can be applied on top of a glaze

Silver, copper and lustred porcelain.
Kerry Richardson, 1998.

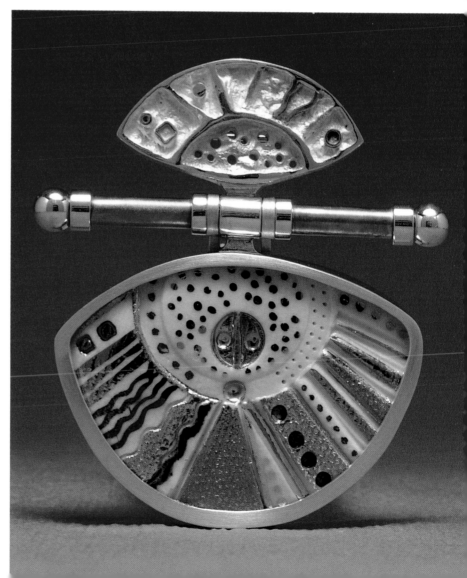

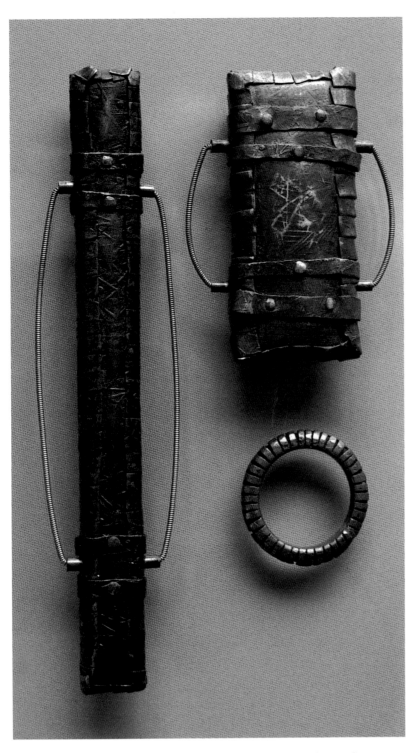

Wrapped copper brooches and rings. This was a student project and the pieces were completed without any soldering. Elizabeth Haynes.

using enamels and lustres. This is a very simplified explanation of how to use porcelain – ceramics is an ancient and complex discipline about which there is a huge amount of technical knowledge. However, the combination of porcelain and metal works well and is worth trying.

There are also various coloured clays sold for jewellery that harden in a domestic oven. Although this material suffers from a rather amateur image it has the potential to be used in a much more interesting and experimental way. The way in which this material is often used demonstrates that it is the idea that is more important than the material.

COPPER

A pinkish-coloured metal, copper is easy to work as it is very soft. Anneal it in the same way as silver by heating to dull red heat and then quenching in water. As it is so soft it is not a good choice for anything structural unless it is used in thick sections. Copper is cheap and easily available in all sorts of forms. Most model shops sell sheet rod and tubing and although this is an expensive way to buy copper it is very convenient. Copper can be silver soldered and cleaned and polished in the same way as silver. It tarnishes very quickly so if you want to keep a particular effect you need to seal the surface from the air as soon as you have finished. A matt lacquer or wax will prevent the copper from oxidizing. Copper can be patinated easily; oxidizing with liver of sulphur turns it black, that when burnished looks like haematite. Other simple patination techniques include using horse's urine to colour the copper green. If you know someone who owns a horse, particularly if they are stabled on wood shavings, ask for a bag of soggy wood shavings and bury the copper in it for a few days. Heating the copper and quenching will bring up some beautiful reds particularly if the surface is covered with FM solution first. Quenching in hot water will produce purplish shades. The colours seem to develop best on metal that has not been heated before and of course if you subsequently heat it the colours will change, so you need to plan ways to connect pieces without heat if this is the surface effect you are seeking. As with the polished metal, patination needs to be protected from the air with a lacquer of wax as soon as the desired effect has been reached.

Enamelled copper wire is made for the electrical industry although the suppliers helpfully also recognize its potential for use in jewellery. Because the wire has a coloured surface you cannot heat it or polish it. If you are incorporating it with precious metal you need to have finished the precious metal parts of the piece before adding the copper wire. It is very soft to work, will lend itself to most textile techniques and it comes in various colours and thicknesses, 0.5mm and 0.3mm are the most useful thicknesses.

EGYPTIAN PASTE

Believed to have been first used by the ancient Egyptians before 5000BC for jewellery and small tomb figures, Egyptian paste is clay that incorporates the glaze within the body and is best used for small simple items. The less the clay is handled, the better, as it dries out easily. If the clay starts to dry use a small paintbrush to add water a little bit at a time. Shaping with hands or pressing into a small plaster mould are the best methods for working. As the paste dries it forms soda crystals on the surface that when fired melt and harden into a glaze and in its best known form is a bright turquoise.

Weigh the ingredients carefully and transfer into a clean plastic bag. Add a small amount of water (maximum 2 tablespoons to 100g of powder) – too much water will result in a sloppy mess. Mix by a kneading and pinching movement to the outside of the bag until a stiff paste is

achieved. The quantity in this recipe will produce a ball of clay about 5cm across.

Soda Feldspar	40g
Flint	20g
China clay	15g
Ball clay	5g
Sodium bicarbonate	6g
Soda ash	6g
Whiting	5g
Fine white sand	88g
Bentonite (for extra plasticity)	2g

To give the coloured surface add one of the following:

Copper carbonate: 2% for turquoise
Cobalt carbonate: ¼–1% for blue
Chromium oxide: ½–1% for green
Manganese dioxide: 1–6% for mauve to brown.

While the pieces are drying out the soda can be seen growing into crystals. It is important not to touch these as this will result in sections of the piece losing the glaze, so it is important to move them into the firing position early. If you are making beads they will need to be strung on some kiln wire to be fired, before the crystals grow. Support the beads on a wire between two kiln supports or firebricks. Other items need to be placed on a clean kiln shelf or unglazed ceramic tile with a recognized kiln wash to stop them sticking to the surface during the firing. When the clay is dry and the glaze fully formed, fire in a kiln to 980°C (as with all ceramic firings start with the kiln cold).

EXOTIC NUTS AND SEEDS

There are several sorts of exotic seed that can be carved. They are very hard and close-grained and will take very detailed and fine carving. For carving use pendant drill burrs, files and small knives or gravers (engraving tools).

SAFETY

Always wear an appropriate mask and possibly gloves when handling dry ceramic materials. Ceramic oxides (particularly chromium oxide) are poisonous.

Pendant with interchangable fabric insert.
Shelby Fitzpatrick, 1999.

Vegetable Ivory

Vegetable ivory comes from the nut of a South American palm (*Phytelephas macrocarpa*). The nut contains a clear fluid that gradually becomes milky and as hard as ivory. It was often used in the manufacture of buttons before plastics were developed.

Tagua or wild orange nut and the **Uxinut** are also suitable for carving.

FABRICS AND THREADS

All sorts of fabrics can be used in jewellery, look in specialist theatre shops for exotic textures and colours. There is a very useful liquid available from good fabric retailers that when painted along the edge of a piece of fabric seals the edge and stops it fraying.

Silk can be painted with specialist silk paints.

Sugar and water solution, PVA or starch can stiffen a fabric.

Synthetic materials used for sail making and kites are great as they do not fray and have a certain amount of stiffness enabling them to hold their shape.

FEATHERS

Feathers have been used extensively in jewellery for centuries. They are surprisingly strong and can be washed in mild shampoo and dried with a hair drier. Peacock feathers, particularly if just the iridescent fronds are used individually, work well. Ostrich, Marabou and Guinea Fowl feathers can be

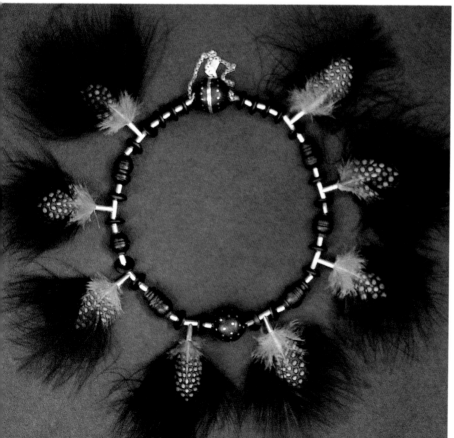

Feather necklace. Silver, turned and inlaid ebony, black marabou and green guinea fowl feathers. Sarah Macrae, 1986.

dyed with fabric dyes or can be bought commercially ready dyed.

FOUND OBJECTS

Try incorporating shells, bones (fish or bird bones are particularly good), fossils, industrial offcuts and waste, old watch parts, children's toys such as lego (as well as the bricks there are all sorts of interesting shapes particularly in some of the space ship sets), pebbles, electrical components. There are many small found objects that lend themselves to being part of a piece so keep your eyes open. The American jeweller Robert Ebendorf uses assemblage incorporating photographs and instrument dials amongst other things, creating interesting new relationships.

GOLD

Gold is arguably the most beautiful, ductile and malleable metal available for jewellers to work. The main reason it has been valued by people throughout history is because of its visual and tactile qualities, its colour and shine, the unchanging qualities, it does not oxidize or corrode and because of its rarity. It was one of the earliest metals to be worked, only copper was used earlier than gold.

Pure gold (24kt) is soft and very malleable, too soft to make anything structural but it can be used for decoration and for the bezels of rub-over settings where the colour can provide some fantastic contrasts.

To give it strength gold is alloyed with other metals, usually silver and copper. The lowest-quality gold generally used by jewellers is 9kt, that is, 9 parts gold out of 24 parts. 9kt yellow gold is a hard and dirty metal to work, good for structural strength but it oxidizes when heated. It should be left to air cool after heating as sudden quenching can shatter the metal. 9kt is also produced in red, green and white, of which the green is too soft for anything but decoration. 9kt white gold has a slightly warmer colour than silver and is a strong and useful metal. Pieces combining 9kt white with 18kt yellow can be very effective.

For colour and strength with malleability 18kt yellow gold is the most beautiful metal to work. It stays very clean, it does not oxidize when heated and polishes easily. White gold of 18kt is, however, a cold grey-white colour similar to platinum and is very strong and good for fine intricate work. These are some of the more usual gold karats and colours but

Feather brooch. Different colour gold. Robert Feather.

there are many more and each bullion dealer's alloys will vary slightly in colour as will the alloys they stock. The Europeans do not use 9kt but mainly 14kt gold. Other more unusual alloys include 20kt rose gold, a warm pinky-coloured gold that is much harder than expected for a high karat gold. Blue gold is another unusual colour that is sometimes available.

Each karat and colour of gold has its own solder in different melting points (hard, medium or easy) so that a good join should be virtually invisible. It is particularly important if the piece is to be sold, and therefore hallmarked, that the correct karat solder is used. In cases where a higher karat gold is being used as additional decoration on a piece, the solder used can be of the lower karat as it is the lower karat that determines the hallmark. For example, a 9kt white gold piece with 18kt yellow decoration can be soldered with 9kt white gold solder as the piece will be hallmarked 9kt. The hallmarking law also states that in this situation the higher karat gold should not exceed fifty per cent of the total weight of the piece. When working in gold remember to carefully save all the tiny bits of scrap and dust from filing (known as lemel) as it can be remelted for decoration or saved and sold back to the bullion dealers.

PAPER

Paper can be cut, folded, woven or moulded. The variety of paper available is extraordinary – from thick hand-made Indian paper to gossamer-fine Japanese tissue papers, from highly textured to satiny smooth. As well as using ready-made papers you can also experiment with moulding paper pulp into a plaster mould.

To make the mould:
◆ Make a shape out of plasticine. Avoid any undercuts or you will not be able to remove the paper forms from the mould.
◆ Place the plasticine shape in the bottom of a plastic tub. Make sure it is secured to the bottom or it will float off when you pour the plaster in.

Necklace. 18kt gold and baroque pearls.
Jeanne Werge-Hartley, 1977.

- Mix some plaster of Paris (add plaster of Paris to water until it forms peaks of plaster above the surface, gradually mix with your hand below the surface so that you do not introduce lots of air bubbles.
- Pour over the plasticine model.
- When the plaster has set remove from the plastic tub, take out the plasticine model and leave the plaster to dry out thoroughly (24 hours somewhere warm).

To make the pulp:
- Tear up strips of a good quality rag paper and soak in water overnight.
- Liquidize in a mixer until you have a fine pulp.
- Using a fine paintbrush build up a thin even layer of paper pulp inside the mould.
- When the whole of the inside of the mould is covered, blow-dry with a hair dryer. You can join forms together with pulp to make total hollow forms.
- Paint with shellac to harden.

PLASTICS

Plastic is a generic term that covers an enormous range of materials made with vastly different qualities for a wide variety of industries. Acrylic and Polyester Resin are two of the types of plastic available to be used by jewellers. Nylon and polypropylene are also used.

Acrylic

Acrylic has a feeling of quality about it due to its weight, and its relative hardness allows it to be used for crisp and precise shapes. Known as perspex (or plexiglass in the USA) it is available in sheet, rod and tube in a wide variety of thicknesses and sizes. It is produced in transparent or opaque colours, in ultraviolet sensitive colours and in light-collecting rod form. Acrylic can be cut with a saw, filed, shaped and smoothed using the same tools and techniques used for precious

metal although it has a tendency to melt when the tool heats up due to friction. This is particularly a problem when using techniques like sawing and drilling as the tool will stick as soon as you pause and the acrylic resets. It helps to keep the acrylic and the tool wet. When turning on a lathe, which causes a rapid build-up of heat due to friction, it is best to keep a steady flow of water over the work. A useful tool for rough shaping is a cintride file or for smaller, more intricate shapes, use a burr attachment in a pendant drill. Old or cheap files are best

Brooch. Paper formed in a plaster mould trapped and riveted between pieces of anodized aluminium. Suzanne Hampson.

Acrylic penannular brooch. Turned and carved acrylic finished with pumice and Scotchbrite. Sarah Macrae, 2000.

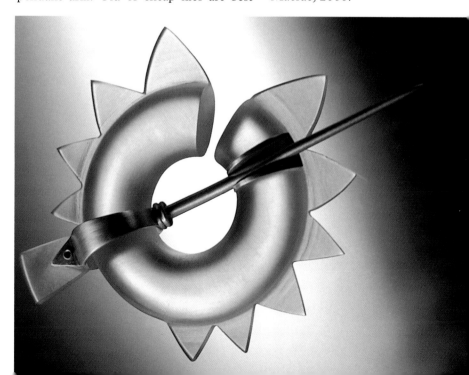

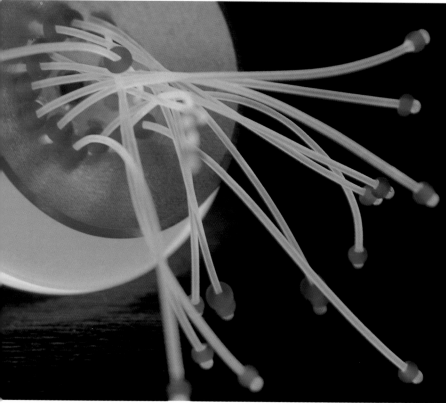

ABOVE: Necklace and earrings in perspex and nylon. Alison Baxter, 1997.

LEFT: UV responsive jewellery. Chris Lockyer.

used as the acrylic tends to clog the surface and ruins them fairly quickly. Finish with silicon carbide papers using them wet. Keep rinsing the residue from the surface of the acrylic and the paper. Polishing can be done with a (clean) polishing mop using 'Hyfin', a white polish, but care must be taken not to overheat and melt the surface of the acrylic. Hand polishing can be done with either perspex polish or 'autosol', a chrome polish available from auto repair shops. Acrylic takes a matt or satin finish very well and can be sandblasted or finished with pumice and Scotchbrite (*see* Chapter 6).

Polyester Resin
Polyester Resin is produced as a thick glutinous liquid and needs to be mixed with 1

per cent of a catalyst (methyl ethyl ketone peroxide) to turn solid. There are various different types of resin but the one most applicable to jewellery is clear-casting or embedding resin. Resin can be coloured with opaque and transparent pigments produced specially for colouring resin and there is also a range of fillers in metallic form such as copper, brass, bronze and iron and others such as slate and synthetic onyx powder. Resin can be mixed with other things like net, lace, glitter, tissue, inks, pure pigments and so on. Being a liquid, resin needs to be contained in a mould while it cures. The mould can either be precisely made to the shape that you require or can be a rough container to hold about the right amount of resin that you can go on shaping after it has cured. Moulds can be made from plaster of Paris, wood, clay or Vinamould/Gelflex (a flexible rubber that has to be heated in a special melting pot) or RTV (room temperature vulcanizing) silicone rubber. The last two enable multiple casts from the same mould. Resin can also

be poured into plastic or foil containers or vacuum-formed shapes. What is best depends on what you are trying to achieve and what facilities you have available.

Resin comes in 1kg or 5kg tins and has a shelf-life of about 3 months. The catalyst comes in a special dropper bottle that allows you to measure precisely the amount needed.

A useful way to check precisely how much resin you need is to fill the mould with water and then pour the water into a measuring jug. Multiply the amount in ml by the specific gravity of resin (1.13) which will give you the weight in grams. Divide by 100 to give 1% and this will give you the weight of catalyst needed. Twenty-two drops of catalyst weigh 1g.

EXAMPLE $130\text{ml} \times 1.13 \text{ (SG)} = 146.9\text{g}$
146.9g divided by 100 = 1.469g
$1.469 \times 22 = 32.318\star$
($\star$round up to 33)

130ml of resin needs 33 drops of catalyst.

RESIN FUMES

Resin fumes are unpleasant and even in low concentrations can cause headaches and nausea. Although using resin is not particularly hazardous, there is some potential risk in continual exposure. Use in a well-ventilated area and do not leave resin curing in an area where you are working.

Resin and its catalyst are highly inflammable, so do not use near a naked flame and store separately in a cool, dark place.

'The Gold of Eldorado II' neckpiece. Knitted and dyed pigmented nylon with gold leaf. Nora Fok, 1997.

Platinum and lapis lazuli bangle with hollow constructed platinum bead. Shelby Fitzpatrick, 1997.

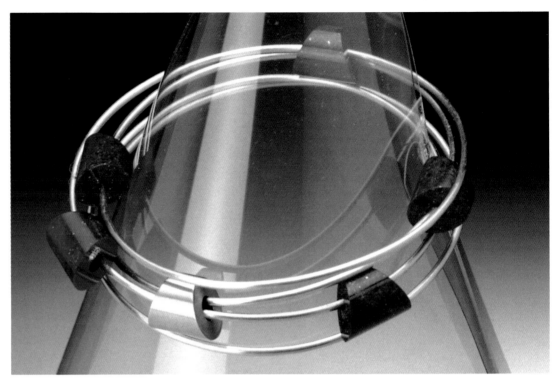

BELOW: *Platinum and pure gold with cloisonné enamel over roller printed platinum.* Jeanne Werge-Hartley, 1999.

Then pour the water into a clean jam jar and mark the level on the jar with a spirit marker pen. Pour the water away and dry the inside of the jam jar. Pour in resin to the marked level, add catalyst and stir slowly being careful not to whisk air into the resin. Add colour or other materials if required, and pour into mould. N.B. Never use polystyrene drinks cups to mix resin as they will dissolve and make a sticky mess.

PLATINUM

The most expensive material available for jewellers to work in, platinum, is a whitish grey metal. It is easily contaminated when hot so it is important that all tools and working surfaces (particularly firebricks) are kept very clean. Before platinum is heated it should be cleaned in dilute hydrochloric acid to ensure there is no risk of contamination. At high temperatures platinum can absorb almost anything and once contaminated it is ruined. Its major advantage is its relative strength so that platinum can be used for very delicate ideas. To anneal platinum properly it needs to be held at red heat for about two minutes and then orange heat for 30 seconds. When it is annealed it is extremely ductile but when work-hardened it is strong and springy. An example to illustrate this is that if you tied a knot in a piece of silver wire and pulled on either end with pliers to tighten it, the wire would start to stretch before the knot was fully tight. With platinum, however, the knot would tighten before the wire would stretch.

To solder platinum to platinum with platinum solder either an oxygen flame or a micro weld needs to be used. However, if the design incorporates gold with platinum, then gold solder can be used and the heat generated by a French blowtorch is sufficient. Gold solder melts at a much lower temperature; it is, therefore, too low to risk contaminating the platinum. Polishing can take place before pieces are soldered together because platinum does not form any fire scale when heated. Hand polishing needs to be particularly thorough working through all grades of silicon carbide paper changing direction all the time. Machine polish with porthos and diamond paste.

PMC (PRECIOUS METAL CLAY)

PMC is one of the newest, most exciting materials available to jewellers. It consists of

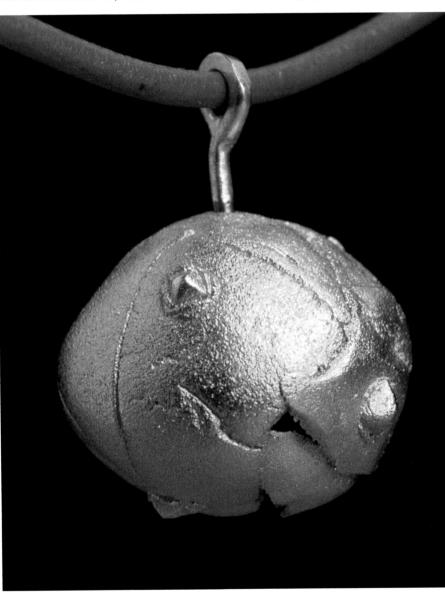

Gold precious metal clay bead pendant. Tim McCreight, 1995.

very fine particles of metal mixed with an organic binder and water. When PMC is fired in a kiln the water and binder burn out leaving 100 per cent pure assayable precious metal. Developed and made by the Japanese company Mitsubishi Materials Corporation, it is available in pure silver, pure gold, pure platinum and 18kt gold yellow, red and white. It is more expensive than conventional metal but the possibilities for its use are fascinating.

PMC is a soft clay, a bit like children's modelling clay to work with. It can be rolled out into a sheet, cut and joined, stretched, folded, squeezed and pinched. Forget about metal being hard, PMC needs you to think in a slightly different way. It is a good idea to experiment with some ideas in something like children's modelling clay. Try to work with the material and use its plastic qualities rather than having a fixed idea that you are trying to work to. The advantage that PMC has over casting is the immediacy and direct contact with the material. It also shrinks when fired by about 50 per cent without losing any detail, making any decoration finer and more delicate.

PMC needs very few tools and equipment apart from a kiln with a pyrometer. Tools useful for working the clay include:

- a small (A4) sheet of acrylic (perspex) or glass to roll the clay out on;
- some polythene to put underneath and on top of the clay to stop it sticking;
- a sharp knife for cutting;
- a childs' plastic rolling pin (or a short length of plastic piping);
- some strips of acrylic (perspex) or wood of different thicknesses to put either side of the clay when rolling out to keep the thickness even;
- some olive oil to put on your fingers to stop the clay sticking to them;
- any small wooden or plastic implements you can find, lolly or cocktail sticks, plastic spatulas, anything that you have available for shaping and smoothing;
- jar of water and a fine paintbrush.

PMC is sold well-wrapped in clingfilm and sealed in a plastic container. As it dries out quite quickly it is best to unwrap only what you need to use and to have a jar of water and a paintbrush ready to add very small amounts of water to the clay to keep it pliable – if you use too much it will become slimy and difficult to handle.

Once you have finished manipulating the clay, allow it to dry out until it reaches a stage known to potters as leather-hard when it is no longer able to be squeezed but can still be cut and smoothed. At this point the form can be refined and smoothed.

Silver precious metal clay and amber pens.
Tim McCreight, 1995.

LEFT: *Imprinted precious metal clay pendant with pleated 1715 hardenable silver fired together.*
BELOW: *Imprinted precious metal clay fish with 1715 hardenable silver wire fired as complete units.* Both pieces, Jeanne Werge-Hartley, 1999.

When it is completely dry it is fragile but can be sanded. Silver PMC is fired at 900°C for about two hours (gold at 1,000°C). The temperature is very important (if the kiln goes over 950°C the silver PMC will melt). It is worth checking the accuracy of your pyrometer with a ceramic cone (these are designed to melt at a specific temperature). The length of time is not so crucial, although it is always better to leave it in the kiln longer than you need to be sure that it is totally fired. When the clay comes out of the kiln it has a slightly velvety surface due to the porosity and is completely white. It can be left to cool or quenched in water. It will also have shrunk by 50 per cent in size due to losing the binder and water. It can be finished in the same way as conventional metal by using burnishers or abrasives.

Although the silver clay is pure silver when fired it is not as soft as pure silver would normally be. Also because of the way the metal bonds in the kiln it is more porous than conventional metal and therefore lighter for its size. It can be soldered conventionally although because of the porosity it is important to withdraw the heat immediately the solder flows or the PMC tends to soak up the solder and the join will fail. It can also be combined with other materials such as ceramic clay and enamel, and synthetic stones and other materials that can withstand the temperature of the kiln can be set directly into the surface before firing. Tim McCreight in the USA has been researching the potential of PMC and has produced a book and video (*see* Further Reading).

REFRACTORY METALS

So called because they are resistant to change, their main use in jewellery has been for their ability, when anodized, to refract light so that the surface appears to be coloured. Anodizing is a process where the metal to be coloured becomes the anode in an electrical circuit suspended in a weak acidic solution. The colour produced varies according to the amount of voltage passed through the metal. The higher the voltage the thicker the anodized layer which splits the light hitting the surface producing the illusion of colour. Butterfly's wings and pools of oil on water produce the same effect. Titanium, niobium and tantalum each have a different colour range. None of the refractory metals can be soldered so mechanical methods of connecting such as riveting or friction fitting need to be used. Annealing is also only possible with highly sophisticated equipment in a vacuum. Anne Marie Shillito who is a leading authority on the use of refractory metals has been developing ways of using laser cutting in jewellery.

Titanium

Probably the refractory metal most people are familiar with, titanium is a very hard, relatively light but strong metal. Care should be taken not to damage your tools when working with this metal as it is harder than the steel of the tools. Files in particular are quickly ruined. To saw titanium use a fine saw blade, between a 4/0 and a 5/0. Titanium can be anodized electrolytically or coloured by heating with a torch. The very brightly coloured titanium jewellery in the high street has been etched in hydrofluoric acid prior to anodizing which brings out the really strong colours. Hydrofluoric acid is a highly dangerous acid and should never be used without stringent safety precautions including a fume cupboard and protective clothing. Heat-colouring titanium is much more subtle and with practice blues, pinks and golds can be achieved. The amount of heat needed is quite small and it is fairly easy to get the metal too hot too quickly and go beyond the colour range. Titanium will also hot forge (heat to orange heat and form using hammers on an anvil).

Niobium

Niobium is a pale grey metal that is much softer than titanium. It can be shaped, curved and bent and wire can be pulled down through drawplates. It can be coloured electrolytically in the same way as titanium but it cannot be heat coloured. The range of colours in niobium includes gold, blue, pink and green.

Tantalum

Tantalum is the heaviest of the three refractory metals and is dark grey in colour. The weight gives the metal a greater feeling of quality and it is the softest of the three enabling a considerable amount of shaping, curving or bending to take place. The colours on tantalum are particularly intense blues and pinks.

All three refractory metals can be polished and if a high shine is required it is particularly important to work through the grades of silicon carbide papers and/or garriflex before machine polishing with tripoli and rouge. The colour on the metal is much more intense when the surface is matt or satin-finished (*see* Chapter 3).

The colouring can be controlled by anything that prevents the build-up of the anodized layer. Waterproof etching tape, photo resist, self-adhesive plastic, etching stop out, wax crayons or grease have all been used with success. Resists can be used

in two ways – in either most of the metal can be covered only leaving exposed the area intended for the highest voltage. The resist can then be removed in parts for each subsequently lower voltage or the whole piece can be anodized to the lowest voltage and then the areas required to be this colour covered with resist before anodizing to the next voltage. Another possibility is to anodize to a high voltage and then to remove the layer in places. A burr in a pendant drill works effectively – the metal can then be anodized again at a lower voltage.

This can be repeated until a rich pattern is developed.

SILVER

Silver is produced in a range of alloys that have different characteristics, advantages and disadvantages. Standard silver is the most commonly used alloy and is produced in a large range of different thicknesses of sheet, wire and tube. The thickness of precious metal is usually measured in gauges or millimetres.

Brooch. Anodized niobium and titanium. Designed using CAD (Computer Aided Design) and made using laser cutting. Ann Marie Shillito, 1994/5.

GAUGE	1	2	3	4	5	6	7	8	9	10	11	12	13	14	15
mm	0.2	0.25		0.3	0.35	0.4	0.5	0.55	0.6	0.7	0.8	0.9	0.95	1.1	1.2

GAUGE	16	17	18	19	20	21	22	23	24	25	26	27	28	29	30
mm	1.3		1.5		1.65		1.85	2.1	2.2	2.4	2.6	3.0	3.2	3.5	4.0

Necklace. 1715 hardenable silver and enamel. Jeanne Werge-Hartley.

Pure Silver

Pure silver is very soft with little strength and is only useful for decoration unless being used in large volume. The only possible exception might be a piece of tight weaving where the flexibility would be an advantage and the bulk of the weaving would give strength. Anneal to dull red heat and quench.

Standard Silver

The basic all-purpose alloy in which copper has been added to the pure silver to give it strength and hardness. The main disadvantage is that the copper oxidizes when standard silver is heated producing firestain in the surface of the metal. This layer of copper oxide has to be removed before polish-ing or it shows as a pale grey cloud in the polished surface. *See* Chapter 4 for ways of preventing and removing firestain.

1715 Hardenable Silver

This is an alloy that has been made for about 30 years that as the name suggests can be irreversibly hardened. It was first developed by Johnson Matthey but is now produced by Cooksons. 1715 does not contain any copper so there is no firestain. It is produced in a limited range of sheet and wire. It can be bought as two types – 'P' quality, this is pre-hardened and is as hard as hard drawn silver. This cannot be annealed and so is useful for pins or enamelling or for any situation where the metal does not need to be shaped and you want strength without firestain. The other is 'N' quality that can be annealed and shaped. It should be annealed in a kiln (800°C with the door shut to exclude air for about 1min), however it is also possible to anneal with a torch at a slightly lower temperature than you would anneal standard. When all shaping and forming is complete but before any soldering is done the 1715 needs to be hardened. This is done in a kiln at 800°C in air (the door of the kiln needs to be slightly ajar) for 2 hours per 1mm of thickness. When the pieces come out of the kiln they are permanently hardened and are covered in a white oxide. The white oxide forms whenever the 1715 is heated and it must be removed from around the join every time you solder or the solder join will be weak.

Because the metal is so strong in its hardened state it is not good to rely on butt joints; when you bend a butt join in standard silver the metal either side of the join will bend before the join – if you do the same with 1715, the join will give before the metal on either side bends. It is better always to overlap or interlock the joins to give additional strength. Despite this alloy needing a bit more thought when using, its advantages in terms of its strength and lack of firestain make it an ideal metal particularly for enamelling and for fine work.

SLATE

Slate is a dark grey stone that forms in layers. Old roofing slates are a good source. Slate can be cut with a jeweller's saw, filed

Silver and slate earrings. Carlo Verda, 1998.

Three carved stone penannular brooches. Silver and soapstone; Silver and alabaster; Silver and fired (1,080°C) soapstone. Sarah Macrae, 1994.

and polished with silicon carbide paper and tripoli and rouge. It can also be carved with burrs in a pendant drill.

STEEL

There are many different types of steel – for example, mild, stainless, silver and tool steel, all with their own characteristics. Mild is relatively soft and tool is very hard. Stainless steel and silver steel are probably the most suitable for jewellery. Steel can be sawn, filed and polished but because of its hardness it will damage tools such as files fairly quickly. Steel hot-forges easily.

STONE

Soft Stones

There are a number of English soft stones that are suitable for use in jewellery that are easy to carve, and do not need to be shaped by specialist lapidary tools, but since they are fairly fragile, shapes cannot be too delicate.

Alabaster

Alabaster is a white or sometimes pink translucent stone that will polish to a high shine. It will shape easily with a cintride file or burrs in a pendant drill. Silicon carbide papers used wet are good for finishing but avoid getting the alabaster too wet as it tends to absorb water. After the finest silicon carbide papers have been used, finish with a fine beeswax polish.

Soapstone

English soapstone is a greeny colour although if you fire it in a kiln to about 1,080°C (ceramic biscuit firing) it turns the stone dark red. Soapstone, like alabaster, can also be shaped easily with a cintride file or burrs on the pendant drill and finished with silicon carbide papers and wax.

Ancaster

Ancaster is a soft creamy white and often contains fossils and mica.

Necklaces. Silver and gold with carved soapstone and alabaster beads. Harriet St Leger, 2000.

Necklace. Sterling silver and Chinese turquoise rondelle beads etched and oxidized. Elizabeth Maldonado, 1995–96.

Precious and Semi-Precious Stones

Diamonds, emeralds, sapphires and rubies are classified as precious stones and all others as semi-precious. Sapphire and ruby are the same stone, called corundum, sapphires ranging in colour from white through yellow and green to blue and pink, and rubies being deeper pink to red. Diamonds are also found in different colours, some of the rarest being the pinks that are mined in Australia. Stones are cut and sold for setting in jewellery in many different forms. Both faceted and cabochon stones are produced in many unusual shapes, triangular, star, heart, pyramid and bullet as well as the obvious round, oval or square.

MATERIALS

Necklace. Jet with diamond on frosted rock crystal. Vivian Pare, 1999.

BELOW: *Necklace. 18kt gold with opal and pearls.* Jane Farnham, 1984.

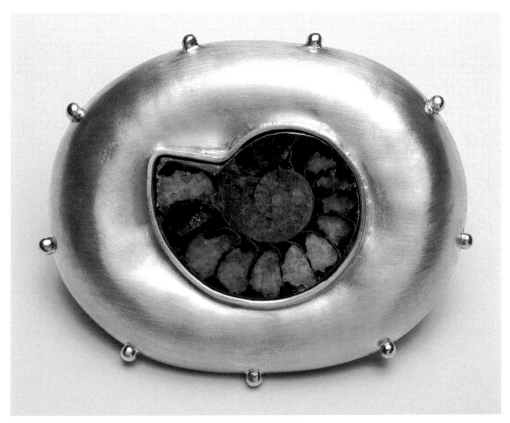

Brooch. Fossilized ammonite set in silver with 18kt beads. Alison Richards, 1999.

BELOW: Brooch. 18kt white gold, agate and diamonds. Abigail Fleissig, 1999.

You can buy natural crystals or slices through natural crystals and beads in every sort of stone. It is worth visiting one of the specialist lapidary fairs that are held in different parts of the country where there is usually a fantastic choice.

WOOD

The best types of wood to use for jewellery are dense close-grained ones that come under the heading of exotic hardwoods. Wood is produced in some interesting forms for fine cabinetmakers and musical-instrument makers. There are beautiful veneers (very thin sheets) and special decorative strips made for inlay that could be used in jewellery. Fingerboards are small planks intended, as the name suggests, for the fingerboards of musical instruments. Wood can be turned on a lathe, sawn with a jeweller's saw, if the pieces are small, or with a tenon (woodworker's saw) if larger. Another accurate saw that I find very useful is a pull saw (from B&Q). Fixing pieces together can be done with wood glue. The pieces should be clamped tightly together in a vice or with G clamps until the glue is dry. Alternatively pieces can be riveted (*see* Chapter 5). Files can be used to shape pieces and fine sandpaper to smooth working with the direction of the grain. Fine wire wool or garriflex work well to finish the surface and if you want a glossy surface use a good quality beeswax polish.

Ebony

Ebony is an almost black tight-grained hardwood. Because of its hardness it will take a considerable amount of fine detail. If polished to a high shine with beeswax it can look almost like stone.

Reversible hairpin. Roller-printed silver with turned ebony. Sarah Macrae, 1994.

Padauk
A deep red wood that is bright orange when first cut.

Rosewood
A dark red/brown.

Purple Heart
A rich purply/brown.

Lignum Vitae
White with a waxy feel when finished.

Tulipwood
Red stripy patterned.

Boxwood
Pale, very close-grained wood with delicate grain pattern.

Four penannular brooches contained in an ebony box. Brooches are made of ebony, acrylic, alabaster and silver with bullet-shaped blue topaz set at the ends of the pins. Sarah Macrae, 2000.

PROJECT ONE

A PAIR OF HAIRPINS

OPPOSITE PAGE:
Acrylic, silver and feather hairpins. 2001.

The length of a hairpin is a personal choice and it does depend on how much of and how heavy the hair is. Generally though the pin should be between 100mm and 300mm long and between 3mm and 10mm thick. They do not need to be identical, or even the same size to work.

Materials

- Acrylic rod or you could use a coloured plastic knitting needle for the main part of the pin, which you can often buy in charity shops.
- Silver or brass tubing of the same external diameter as the material for the pin.
- Feathers.
- Two-part epoxy resin glue (Araldite is a clear two-part epoxy that is very good but it sets very rapidly. Only mix enough for each hairpin at a time and have everything you need ready).
- Methylated spirit and some rag to clean off excess glue.
- Two grades of silicon carbide paper (400 and 1000 grit).
- Scotchbrite (green pan scourer).

Tools

- A jeweller's saw.
- Blades (2/0 or 3/0).
- A large file (a cintride file is useful).
- A pillar needle file.
- Cocktail sticks and a small disposable container to mix glue in.
- If you can borrow a chenier (tubing) cutter it makes cutting the tube and pin straight much easier, but this is not essential.

Hairpins. Roller printed and etched silver with turned ebony. Sarah Macrae, 1992.

1. Cut the acrylic rod or knitting needle to the length you have chosen, the easiest way is to saw it with a jeweller's saw (Fig 2).

2. Using the large file to begin with, then the pillar needle file, file one end to a slightly rounded point and the other end flat (square) (Fig 3).

Fig 1 Coloured knitting needles and acrylic rod.

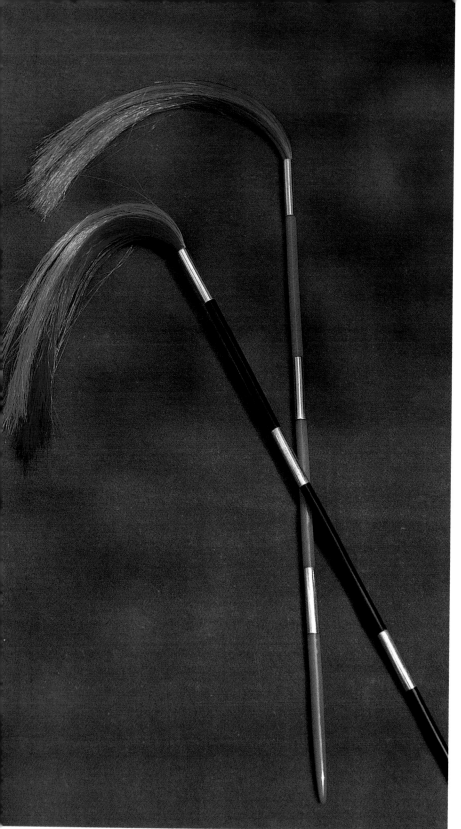

Hairpins. Knitting needles, brass tubing, synthetic hair.
Sarah Macrae, 1981.

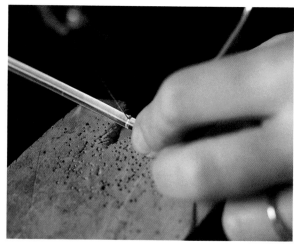

Fig 2 Saw the length required.

Fig 3 File one end to a rounded point and the other square.

Fig 4 Make a small cut around the end of the rod.

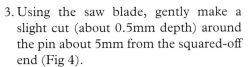

ABOVE: Fig 5 File up to the saw cut so that the end fits inside the tubing.
ABOVE RIGHT: Fig 6 A tight fit.
RIGHT: Fig 7 If it is not a tight fit, gluing becomes more difficult.

3. Using the saw blade, gently make a slight cut (about 0.5mm depth) around the pin about 5mm from the squared-off end (Fig 4).
4. Using the pillar needle file, file round the end of the pin up to the line you have sawn until you have a step that will fit inside the tubing (Fig 5). Try to make this a good tight fit as it will make gluing it together much easier (Fig 6). If it is loose you will need to support the pin while it is gluing to make sure it dries straight (Fig 7).
5. Saw the tubing to the length required. It needs to be at least 15mm for there to be room to glue the pin and feathers but it can be longer if you want it to be (Fig 8).
6. File the tubing flat (square) at both ends (Fig 9).
7. Wash the pin and tubing well to make sure they are clean and free of any grease, and see that you have everything ready to glue (Fig 10).

Chenier (tubing cutter) and chenier vice.

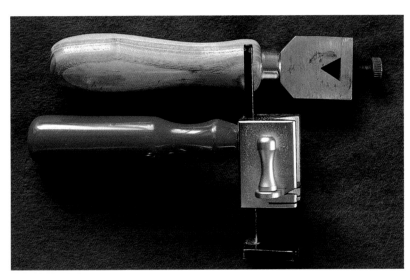

RIGHT: Fig 8 Saw the tubing to the required length.
FAR RIGHT: Fig 9 File the ends square.

BELOW: Fig 10 Ready for gluing.
BOTTOM: Hairpins. Turned acrylic and silver in painted wood box. Sarah Macrae, 2000.

8. Mix the epoxy resin and using a cocktail stick put a thin even layer of glue inside the tubing to a depth of about 5mm; also put a thin film of glue on the step at the end of the pin. Push the pin into the tubing, wipe off any excess glue with a cloth just moistened with methylated spirit and leave to dry.

9. Clean up and finish the pin using silicon carbide paper – first the 400 grit and then 1000 grit. Then holding the (wet) Scotchbrite in one hand round the pin, roll the pin between the fingers and thumb of the other hand while moving it in and out of the Scotchbrite until the pin has a bright even surface.

10. Decide on what kind of feathers and how many you want to put in the end of the hairpin. Put some epoxy resin into the end of the tubing, put a tiny amount onto the ends of the feathers, push the feathers into the end of the tube and leave to dry.

Feathers are remarkably strong and can be washed in mild shampoo and dried with a hair dryer. Look at some of the examples of hairpins and try making several pairs, possibly different colours and different lengths. Think about different 'ends' and vary the proportions or the materials.

How to Wear Hairpins

If you have hair long enough to wear in a ponytail you can wear hairpins. Two hairpins will secure even very fine hair. Hold the hair as if you are making a ponytail. Twist the hair until it twists round on itself to make a bun, wind the tail bits round and hold the bun flat to the back of your head with one hand. Skewer the bun at about 45 degrees from the vertical making sure that the pin goes through from the bun to the hair closest to your head and back out of the bun again. Do the same at the opposite angle with the other pin so that the pins cross in the middle. You should not need anything other than the hairpins to secure the hair.

Hairpin. Turned ebony, feathers and niobium. Sarah Macrae, 1984.

LEFT: Hairpins. Tortoiseshell knitting needles, brass tubing, feather and Japanese paper thread. Sarah Macrae, 1983.

4 BASIC PROCESSES FOR WORKING IN PRECIOUS METALS

This chapter will cover all the basic techniques that you will need to make some simple pieces of jewellery. It also includes the second project, making a silver ring. This project takes you through all the basic techniques. You will learn how to mark out the metal, how to saw, file, anneal, bend, solder, clean up and polish. Once these basics have been understood you can go on adding techniques as your ideas develop.

A TECHNICAL NOTEBOOK

It is a good idea to start a technical notebook at this point to record precisely what you have done at each stage. If you get into a routine of writing down what you do it will make things easier when you start to form your own ideas.

PREPARING THE METAL

Marking out

To start with you will need to transfer a design onto the metal and you can do this in lots of different ways. You can scribe directly onto the surface with a sharp point. Permanent OHP pens will draw straight onto the surface of the metal although it is best to slightly roughen the surface first with Garriflex or Scotchbrite. White paper sticky labels are useful as you can draw directly on to them, you can also transfer a tracing easily. Cover your metal with a white sticky label, trace the design in pencil and then turn the tracing paper over and draw over the traced lines from the back. Turn the tracing paper over again and position on your metal then go over the lines again with pencil from the right side – this will transfer your drawing onto the sticky label. If you use a computer at home you can also scan in a drawing and print it directly onto a sticky label, this can be very useful if you want to alter the scale of the drawing. If you want a very fine accurate line to work to, you can use engineer's blue or a permanent marker pen to cover the area with ink and then scribe through to the metal. In this case, to transfer the design, hold the tracing carefully in position and with a sharp scribe or a needle make a series of pin holes through the tracing so that when you take the tracing away you can join the dots. Another

OPPOSITE: Simple silver rings. Sarah Macrae.

Saw frame.

Snips.

alternative is to paint the metal with process white paint and draw directly onto it.

SAWING

For cutting metal jewellers generally use a piercing saw, so called as you can use it to cut shapes out of the middle of an area of metal. This may seem an awkward tool to use at first but with practice it is a very accurate way to cut shapes out. Cutting with snips may seem easier to the beginner, but because the snips distort and buckle the edge of the metal it is very wasteful in terms of materials. Added to that the amount of time that then needs to be spent filing and cleaning up the edge means that sawing is definitely the quickest way to work. Saw blades are sold in packs of twelve or a gross (144) and come in a range of different thicknesses. A general rule is that there should be three teeth touching the metal at any one time, so the thicker the metal the thicker the saw blade. A 3/0 saw blade is a good general purpose size for most things and a 6/0 is useful for very delicate shapes.

FITTING A SAW BLADE

To fix your saw blade into the frame, make sure the teeth are pointing downwards towards the handle. The saw cuts on the downstroke. Fix one end into the clamp at one end of the frame. Brace the frame between the workbench and your body to compress the frame before fixing the blade into the clamp at the other end. Flick the blade

with a fingernail – if it makes a pinging sound it is OK – if it twangs it is too loose.

When you are ready to start sawing, hold the metal firmly on the bench peg with the line that you are going to saw just clear of the peg. The more secure the metal and the less it flexes as you saw, the easier it is and the less chance you have of breaking the saw blade. It helps to have some beeswax, oil or soap to run the saw blade through to stop it from sticking. Try to keep the blade at right angles to the metal and saw with a steady rhythmic action using the whole blade. It is very tempting to try to rush and put too much pressure on the blade so that the blade bends, the teeth dig in and the blade then sticks and breaks. Be patient.

To saw a shape from the middle of a design you need to drill a small hole in the area you want to remove. Fix the saw blade into one end of the frame. Then thread the saw blade through the hole that you drilled and move the metal up to the end of the frame where the blade is clamped. Now brace the frame and clamp the other end of the saw blade as before.

FILING

As a general rule use the largest file that you can. If you have a lot of filing to do it can help to secure the work in a vice or hand vice to keep your filing accurate. Always file across the short edge otherwise the natural rocking motion of your arm, due to the ball and socket joint at the shoulder, tends to round off the corners. Files are designed to cut in one direction so hold the work firmly against the edge of the bench and file away from you. There is an old jeweller's saying 'File once, look twice' as it is very easy to file off more than you intend to. If you need to file two shapes exactly the same – for instance if you are making earrings – stick the two (or three or four) bits together with double-sided tape and file together.

ANNEALING

Annealing is the process by which the metal is kept soft and malleable. For silver this involves heating the metal to dull red heat, allowing it to air cool to black heat (for small pieces this is only the time it takes to pick up the metal with tweezers) and then cooling by quenching in water. Heat the metal with a soft flame (a reducing flame). Try not to overheat the metal. If you repeatedly take the metal to orange heat rather than dull red the metal will become brittle and difficult to work. It helps to see the colour of the metal if you lower the light levels, either make a contained area of firebricks or turn the lights off. When metal is heated its structure becomes fluid and as it is cooled the pattern of crystals that is formed results in the metal being at its most flexible. If you annealed a piece of silver and then left it, it would stay annealed or soft forever. When the metal is worked (sawn, filed, bent, hammered or whatever) the crystals get more and more broken up and the metal gets harder and more brittle until eventually it breaks (exactly the same as when you bend a piece of wire backwards and forwards until it snaps, that is, metal fatigue). The number of times that a piece needs to be annealed during making depends entirely on how much the metal is being worked. Through experience of the material you learn to judge when annealing is needed. If you are hammering, the resistance in the metal can be felt through the tool, you can feel the hammer bouncing

back off the metal. There is a fine balance to be learnt here as the more often you anneal the metal the more it will oxidize creating more firestain that then takes longer to remove, therefore lengthening the whole cleaning up and polishing process. However, if you do not anneal often enough the metal will crack or even break. Experiment with some scrap bits, and see for yourself what happens.

FIRESTAIN

Fire stain is a grey 'shadow' that is formed just below the surface of standard silver when it is heated. It is caused by the copper content of standard silver oxidizing. If it is not removed it shows through the final polish like a dirty mark. The more the metal is heated the more firestain is caused. There are various ways of dealing with this. Firstly to prevent it forming as much as possible, avoid heating the silver too often or for too long (experience is everything here). There are various commercially available preparations that reduce the amount of firestain. Argotect is one that comes as a powder that is then

Files.

SAFETY

Important rule when improvising or experimenting is to *think*: is this likely to damage me, the tools, or the work in any way?

FIRESTAIN

To check for firestain cover the silver with a piece of tracing paper. You will see any grey areas of firestain more clearly.

PROTECTING YOUR WORK

Protect your work as much as possible while making. The less marks and scratches you put in while you are making the less time the polishing takes. Silver often comes with a protective film covering the surface, leave this on until you have to heat the metal. Cover tools such as pliers and vulnerable areas of silver with masking tape (don't forget to take it off before heating). Scraps of leather can be used to protect the silver from the jaws of tools. Use aluminium or rubber jaw protectors when holding work in a vice. Cleaning up and removing any scratches as you go rather than leaving it all to the end makes the final cleaning up and polishing easier.

mixed with methylated spirits and painted on the work. FM solution works very well. For further information on removing firestain *see* under 'cleaning up' later in this chapter.

PICKLING

Even if you are using FM solution you will need to pickle the work at least once, during making, to clean it. Solder will not flow if the silver is dirty. This involves immersing the work in a solution to remove fire scale (not firestain) from the surface of the metal. Generally jewellers use one of the following three depending on their own personal circumstances and preferences. Dilute sulphuric acid (10:1) or Safety pickle (a commercially available pickle that comes as a powder to be mixed with water) or alum (aluminium potassium sulphate). Sulphuric acid is very effective but potentially the most dangerous, so always make sure it is clearly labelled. Keep it in a proper acid jar with a stopper. Have the stopper ready and close the jar as soon as you have dropped the warmed (not too hot or there is a danger that the acid will spit) piece into the acid. Safety pickle, so called because the fumes are less dangerous than sulphuric acid, is only effective if kept warm. A heat-proof dish with a lid supported on a tripod with a nightlight underneath is very effective. Alum too can be used like this and is a lot safer if a bit slower.

SAFETY

Mixing Acid with Water

Always add acid to water not the other way round. Acid generates heat very quickly when combined with water and if you add water to acid it will provoke a violent reaction. Always work in a well-ventilated area.

BENDING AND SHAPING

Always start with your fingers, move on to wooden formers, leather sandbags and rawhide mallets and then finally, if necessary, metal formers, stakes and hammers. The objective is to achieve the shape you want while marking the metal as little as possible.

To make a sharp bend in a piece of metal, score or file a groove on the side that will become the inside of the bend. File almost all the way through – a line will appear on the other side when you have filed enough. At this point it is really important to anneal the metal, because if you try to bend before

STEEL IN THE PICKLE

Only use brass or plastic tweezers or tongs in the pickle, never steel. Make sure you remove any binding wire before pickling. Steel in the pickle sets up a chemical reaction that deposits a layer of copper onto your work (the work turns pink) – and anyone else's work in the pickle at the time. If this happens you have to physically remove the copper by either bright dipping in nitric acid (diluted to 2:1) or, if the work is too delicate for that, by using an abrasive like Garriflex. Sometimes if you heat the piece up and quench in new clean pickle it will remove the copper. Make sure that you have the pickle in a container with a lid so that the pickle cannot splash you.

you have annealed it will break. After annealing, bend and then run some solder along the inside of the bend to secure it.

Most simple curves for jewellery can be achieved with a brass doming block, wooden doming punches or a swage block. Place the (annealed) metal to be curved into the doming block. Using a punch slightly smaller than the curve in the block, work around the shape hitting the punch with a wooden or rawhide mallet. If you want a deep curve, shape the piece in several stages, starting with a shallow curve. Use the swage block in the same way. You can either cut some lengths of dowelling to lay in the grooves or use the ends of the doming punches. Make sure you never use metal hammers or you will ruin the punches.

A block of lead can be very useful as a surface to support the Silver as you hammer into it. Use steel punches to change the shape. It is important to make sure that the lead does not contaminate the silver as, if heated together, even specks of lead will eat holes in silver. It is usually sufficient to put some paper between the lead and silver.

Repoussé is a more advanced technique where pitch is used to support the work while being shaped with punches from both the front and the back.

Steel silversmithing stakes come in all sorts of interesting shapes and sizes and can be useful if you have access to them.

Improvise – sometimes you can find a shape to work over, door handles, scrap bits of car engine, even flints from the garden can make good formers. There are times when it is better to make a wooden former, carving the shape out of the end grain of a close-grained wood (boxwood is ideal). If you need a longer lasting tool, carve the shape out of some steel stock using stone burrs in the pendant drill, and files, silicon carbide paper and polish to finish.

When curving wire *hold* the wire with pliers at the end and bend with your fingers using the tension in the wire to keep the curve even.

CAPILLARY ACTION SOLDERING

Soldering precious metal is done by capillary action, this means that there is a crossing over and combining of molecules in the join as opposed to lead soldering that is using a lower melting point material to simply 'stick' two pieces of metal together. Silver solder comes in different grades according to its melting point. Enamelling solder is the highest temperature grade and is very close to the melting point of silver. As its name suggests, it is intended to be used to join pieces that are subsequently going to be enamelled and so have to withstand the temperature of an enamelling kiln. The next grade is hard, then medium, easy and extra easy. In a complicated piece with many solder joins it is best to start with a higher grade for the first joins and work down the grades for further joins. Which grades you use is largely a matter of personal preference and what works for you. For less-complicated pieces medium solder can be used throughout. Only use easy or extra easy if it will be the last time you heat the work, or in an emergency repair situation, as

---

SOLDERING

1. Remember solder will not fill or jump gaps. Pieces that are to be soldered need to fit tightly together.
2. Solder does not take any notice of gravity, it will travel up a seam as well as down.
3. Do not place the solder between the two bits to be soldered – it will inevitably go into a lump and you will be left with a gap.

A BAD JOIN

If the join is less than perfect use the saw to saw straight through the join. Removing a saw blade's width of metal will then give a perfect join. If this is not possible use a small piece of wire or a small bit of sheet pushed into the gap, solder in place and file off the excess.

MAKING GRAIN

To practise using the torch and to get used to the temperature at which silver melts, try melting a little scrap of silver (a square millimetre or two). You will find that as it melts it gathers itself up into a perfect ball. Wait for it to spin then pull the flame away slowly allowing it to cool. The tiny ball will have a flat base unless heated in a dip in a charcoal block. There is an ancient method of decoration using grain called granulation.

these solders pit the metal if heated repeatedly. The two surfaces to be joined must be clean and fit tightly together so that if you hold it up to the light, no light should be visible through the join. The solder should be cut up into tiny pieces called pallions and placed touching the join. Solder will not jump gaps or fill holes, however it does defy gravity so when soldering you place the solder where it is easiest to balance it and where, if there is any excess, it is easiest to file off. Sometimes it is easier to balance the work on the solder than the solder on the work. For the solder to flow properly the solder and the area of the join need to be coated in flux. For silver borax is used – it comes either as a powder that you mix to a paste with a small amount of water or as a cone that you grind down to a paste with water in a shallow dish. There are also several recipes for solutions that you can make up that will not only act as a flux but also inhibit the amount of firestain. FM solution (for recipe *see* under Flux and Firestain Inhibitors in Chapter 2) is very effective and easier to use and less messy than borax paste.

Making Clips out of Steel or Titanium

To make clips you need some steel or titanium sheet about 0.5mm thick. Cut a strip about 2–3mm wide and about 35mm long.

1. Bend it in half (Fig 1).
2. Flick one end up with pliers (Fig 2).
3. Again with pliers pull the strip back on itself until the tipped end is parallel with the straight end (Fig 3).

Fig 1 Bend strip in half.

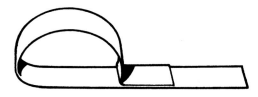

Fig 2 Bend one end up with pliers.

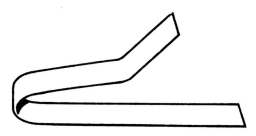

Fig 3 Again with pliers pull the strip back on itself until the tipped end is parallel with the straight end.

These are often so springy that you have to use pliers to lever them on to the pieces you want to hold together.

SOLVING SOLDERING PROBLEMS

Setting up work for soldering often causes problems in terms of balancing and support. The more traditional way of holding complex pieces to be soldered is to set the work partially in plaster of Paris using something like a metal jam jar lid as a base. This is an excellent way to hold things but requires forethought as the plaster needs time to set.

PRE-SOLDERING

In some cases it is helpful to pre-solder if it is particularly difficult to balance the solder in the right place. This means placing the solder on the piece that is to be joined and heating it until it flows over the surface. Rub it down with some silicon carbide paper until it is almost flat and then reheat in position. Watch for a bright line of solder at the edges.

Binding wire is the most usual method. Take a length of wire, double and twist it. Using the wire twisted means that it is less likely that you will solder the wire to your work by accident. It also helps to heat the wire before you use it so that it oxidizes, again so you are less likely to solder it to your work. Use the binding wire as sparingly as you can, if you use too much it will take too much heat away from your work and you will have a problem achieving enough heat for the solder to flow. Don't bind the binding wire too tightly, use a pair of pliers and make 's' shape bends to tighten it so that when the metal expands as it is heated it allows the binding wire to give slightly so that it doesn't cut into the work.

Spring tongs or a third hand are other alternatives. It is also possible to use cotter pins that you can buy or clips that you can make yourself. You can make them out of titanium that has the added advantage of being impossible to solder to anything.

Firebricks can be cut into shape, or slots and grooves cut into them, to support work. It is better to spend ten minutes customizing a piece of firebrick than to spend hours of frustration balancing something that falls over every time you put heat on it. Steel mesh can also be useful and can be shaped to support work. Another very useful material is a modelling clay like 'Darwi' – used in small amounts (pea-sized) it works very effectively to hold pieces in position. If you use a piece bigger than a marble though, it tends to move when heat is applied. Kaowool ceramic fibre sheet is another soldering surface that is soft enough to push the work partially into but is strong enough to support it.

PROTECTING A PREVIOUS SOLDER JOIN

Even if a previous join has been made using a higher grade solder it is sensible to support the join before heating the work for the next one. You can use various materials to stop the solder from running but they still won't prevent the join from collapsing if it is unsupported. Traditionally, powdered Rouge mixed with water or methylated spirit painted over the solder join will stop the solder running but it is very messy and can be difficult to remove. Typing correction fluid works very well, although there is some concern that it is potentially carcinogenic. Clay slip also works. A soft graphite pencil (a 'B' or softer) will stop solder from running over an area where you don't want it. There are also some very good protective pastes like 'Coolheat' that are extremely effective. For example you can reticulate (a controlled melting of the surface) a piece of silver partially covered with paste and the area protected by the paste will stay untouched by the heat.

UNEQUAL VOLUMES OF METAL

One situation that many beginners find difficult is where you need to join two pieces of different volume. For example, to join a small decorative element to a larger piece of sheet. Because the whole of the metal needs to reach the same temperature in order for the solder to flow, the problem arises where the smaller piece of metal gets hotter much quicker than the larger bit. The result is that at best the solder will melt onto the smaller piece as it is pulled towards the hotter metal and at worst that the smaller piece will melt before the larger piece has reached soldering heat. So the task is to even out the heat, to protect or draw away the heat from the smaller bit while exposing the larger bit to greater heat. Raising up the larger bit on a steel mesh can help as not only does the firebrick tend to draw heat away but in raising it up you can direct the flame and heat the larger piece from underneath keeping direct heat away from the smaller piece. At the same time draw the heat away from the

---

BUTT JOINTS

Although solder makes a very strong join, butt joints are to be avoided if possible. If it is feasible to drill a hole to fit a wire in, to overlap or interlock two pieces, then do it. From a design point of view butt joints also often look weak; look at how things around you interconnect, a leaf to a twig, a branch to a tree, a piece of scaffolding to the next bit.

---

smaller piece by using a heat sink. This can be anything that touches the smaller piece, binding wire, spring tongs, a pair of tweezers, or a strip of steel.

CLEANING UP (HAND FINISHING)

The final polish of a piece is entirely dependent on the quality of the hand finishing. This stage can really make the difference between an amateur- and a professional-looking piece of work. There are no short cuts but a wide variety of tools and materials that you can use. The principle is to work from coarse through to fine abrasives making a finer and finer crisscrossing of scratches smoothing the surface until they are so fine that the majority of the light is being reflected back creating a shiny surface.

Abrasives come in many forms (*see* Chapter 3) and which ones you use is a personal choice. Try as many as you can and decide which you prefer. To begin with use silicon carbide paper as it is easily available. How coarse an abrasive you start with largely depends on how marked the surface of the metal is. If there are lots of bad scratches or tool marks on the surface then it is pointless to start with a fine abrasive as it will not get the job done. Start with a coarse (400 or even 240 – the lower the number the coarser the abrasive paper) silicon carbide paper, fold it into a pad or wrap it round something like a piece of wood or the end of a file so that you do not start to wear away the edges of the piece. Thin strips of wood with abrasive papers glued to them are very useful and worth the amount of time it takes to prepare them. Move on to a finer paper grit paper. The split pin attachment on the pendant drill into which you can feed a strip of silicon carbide paper is very useful but as with all power tools be careful that you don't damage your work.

Water of Ayr stone is an abrasive that comes as a stick and is useful for getting into tight spots. It can be filed into the shape you want. Use with water and rub the surface of the metal, keep rinsing away the residue so you can see what you are doing. There are also white glass-fibre sticks that you can use in the same way.

Garriflex is another very useful material, it comes in three grades and is particularly good for removing firestain; it is a rubbery block that can be cut into different shapes with a knife. Powdered pumice is a fine abrasive which can be used on the wrong end of a matchstick.

Polishing threads are good for cleaning difficult-to-reach areas. These are soft cotton threads that can be pinned to the workbench and covered with one of the machine polishing compounds such as Tripoli. The threads (as many as you can fit through the space in the work) are threaded through the piece and it is then moved up and down the strings.

HAND-FINISHING POINTS

◆ If the surface of the metal is badly marked start with an abrasive slightly coarser than the marks.

◆ Keep changing direction as you work (if you work all the time in one direction you will see a 'direction' in the final polish).

◆ Try to keep all the edges and surfaces as crisp and precise as possible, the machine polishing tends to soften all the edges and if they have been rounded during the hand finishing the shapes can end up looking too 'soft'.

Each time you move on to a finer abrasive make sure that there is none of the coarser abrasive left on the work. To be sure it has all been removed, it helps to wash the work in a solution of household ammonia, washing-up liquid and hot water. Hand finishing takes patience, it can take as long to polish a piece as it does to make it, but it makes all the difference to the final appearance of the piece.

MACHINE POLISHING

Machine polishing takes the hand finishing a stage further with even finer abrasive compounds. Again there are many different sorts and grades to choose from. The two most usually used are Tripoli, a reasonably coarse dark yellow compound that is good to start with, followed by a soft rouge to give a very shiny surface. Try out different compounds if you can and make your own choice. Mops for the polisher are made of calico, swansdown, felt or wool. To begin with use a calico mop for tripoli and swansdown for rouge. When you buy new calico or swansdown

mops they need to be 'roughed up' before you can use them or they behave like lots of tiny circular saws. Cut a piece of brass sheet about 60mm × 30mm and then cut one edge with snips into a zig-zag. Push the zig-zag edge into the mop as it is spinning. You end up covered in fluff but you have a lovely soft mop afterwards. When machine polishing, it is really important to keep the different compounds and mops separate so that the finer abrasives do not get contaminated by the coarser ones. Keep the mops separate and dust-free, preferably sealed in a plastic bag. The amount of pressure that you put on the mop with the work is different when polishing with Tripoli from that when polishing with rouge. With the Tripoli push reasonably hard up into the mop but with the rouge use a much softer pressure and wipe the work through the edges of the mop. Always wash the work and your hands in ammonia, washing-up liquid and hot water when changing to a finer compound and when you have finished polishing. (*See* Chapter 6 for some alternatives finishes to a high polish.)

SAFETY

When polishing, stand square on to the polisher and concentrate. Do not allow yourself to be distracted as this is when accidents happen. Always present your work to the bottom quarter of the wheel. Hold the work in your fingers firmly using a pinch grip so that if the work catches in the mop it will not take your fingers with it. Do not entwine your fingers in the work. Wear safety goggles and a dust mask. Do not wear loose clothing or anything that can catch in the polisher, and make sure long hair is tied back.

Polishing. Make sure that you hold the work in a snap release grip so that if the polisher catches the work and snatches it out of your hand it will not damage you. Always work in the bottom quarter of the wheel.

PROJECT TWO

A SILVER BAND RING

The simplest way to learn the basic skills of working with precious metal is to make a silver band ring. This covers all the basic processes fairly quickly and provides a sound foundation on which to build further knowledge. Once you know how to cut the metal out, how to join it and how to finish it you can go on building on your knowledge of the materials and processes. This project should not take very long and the value of the materials is very small, so that if you do make a mistake, it is not too soul-destroying to start again.

For this project you will need the following materials and equipment:

- Piece of 12 gauge silver sheet at least 10mm × 70mm
- Piece of medium silver solder
- Strip of paper
- Pair of dividers
- Cheap paintbrush
- Steel ruler
- Jar of water
- Saw frame
- Packet of 3/0 saw blades
- Beeswax, soap or oil
- Gas torch
- Scribe
- Pillar needle file
- Round steel triblet
- Rawhide mallet
- Pair of snips
- Flux – either borax or FM solution
- Acid jar with dilute (10:1) sulphuric acid or old saucepan and alum
- Two soldering sheets and a soldering block
- Two pairs of tweezers, one brass, one steel
- One pair of half-round, or snipe pliers

- Two sheets of silicon carbide paper (400 and 1000)
- Ammonia and soapy water and a soft brush
- One block of medium Garriflex
- Small piece of tracing paper
- Jar with a mixture of about 1 part household ammonia, 1 part washing-up liquid to about 20 parts hot water (keep the lid on when you are not using it)
- Jeweller's wash brush or clean, soft toothbrush
- Polishing motor* and/or pendant drill
- Polishing compounds – Tripoli and rouge
- Polishing mops – calico and swansdown

* Or, if you have not got access to a polishing motor, a silver polishing cloth.

1. *Measuring*

    Start by measuring the finger for which the ring is intended. Using the strip of paper wind it round the fattest part of the finger (for most people this is the knuckle but for some it is the base of the finger). Fold the strip of paper where it meets round the finger (Fig 1). Err on the side

OPPOSITE: Examples of simple silver rings.

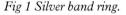

Fig 1 Silver band ring.

of it being too small rather than too big as it is much easier to stretch a ring than to make it smaller.

2. Decide on how wide you want the ring to be and set the dividers to that width.

3. *Marking out*
   Assuming that one edge of your silver sheet is straight, use the dividers to score a line parallel to the edge the width that you would like your ring to be (Fig 2).

4. Using the strip of paper on your piece of silver measure the length of the ring (Fig 3), then with the steel ruler as a guide use the scribe to score a line (Fig 4).

Fig 2 Dividers.

Fig 3 Marking out.

Fig 4 Marking out.

5. *Sawing*
   Run the saw blade through a piece of beeswax or soap, then holding the silver flat onto the workbench with the saw frame upright start to saw along the length of the ring. Try to saw steadily and smoothly with a rhythmic action using the whole blade (Fig 5). If you push too hard, the blade will bend and stick and then break. Saw along the

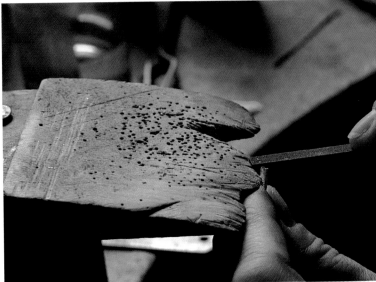

ABOVE: Fig 5 Sawing.
ABOVE RIGHT: Fig 6 Filing.

waste side of your score line so that any wobbles in your sawing will not matter.

6. When you reach the end of the long edge you can either pull the blade back and cut the shorter edge from the outside edge or keep sawing while gently turning the silver until the blade is facing across the strip then continue to saw to the outside edge.

7. *Filing the ends square*
Using the pillar needle file, file across the short edges so that they are straight and square. Don't worry about the long edges at this stage (Fig 6).

8. *Annealing*
The next stage is annealing (Fig 7). If you are using the FM solution, paint the solution over the silver, back and front. Place the strip of silver so that it is leaning on the fire brick. Heat the metal with a reducing flame (that is without too much oxygen). If you are using a French blowtorch blow gently down the air

tube, you are aiming to get rid of as much of the yellow part of the flame as you can without making the flame roar. Keep your lungs topped up with air with little breaths (if you run out of air and then take a deep breath your metal will have gone cold again in the meantime). Heat the metal until you see a red glow

Fig 7 Annealing.

Figs 8 & 9 Forming using fingers.

Fig 10 Forming using snipe pliers.

ABOVE: Fig 11 Push the two ends beyond each other so they overlap, then pull back so they meet.
ABOVE RIGHT: Fig 12 Cutting solder into pallions.

pass over it; it is easier to see this if you are in a poorly lit area so it is helpful to turn the lights off until you have got used to the colour change. When the metal reaches red heat, pick it up with the steel tweezers and quench in a jar of water.

9. *Forming*

When forming metal, the objective is to get to the shape you want and in the process do as little damage as possible to the metal's surface. Start by using your fingers to bend the strip of silver into a ring shape (Fig 8). When bent as far as it will go with fingers, use the snipe pliers to bring the two ends together. Use the pliers to *hold* one end of the strip of silver and use your fingers to bend the metal (Fig 9). Then hold the other end of the strip in the pliers and bring the two ends together (Fig 10). It is helpful to protect the silver from contact with the steel pliers by wrapping the jaws of the pliers with some masking tape. The ends should meet together well enough so that when you hold the metal up to a window you should not be able to see light through the join (Fig 11). Solder will not jump gaps.

10. *Soldering*

Cut the solder into very small bits with the snips; these are called pallions (Fig 12). Paint the ring and the solder with FM solution (Fig 13) or if you are using borax mix to a paste and paint onto the solder and around the join. Remember the FM and the borax are alternatives so you do not need both. Solder does not

Fig 13 Paint the ring with FM solution.

Figs 14 & 15 Soldering.

the centre of the ring. When the metal has reached the right temperature you will see the ring drop as the solder travels up the join in the ring. Quench in water (Fig 15).

11. *Pickling*

At this point you may need to 'pickle' the ring if it looks dirty. Pickling is not always necessary if you have used the FM solution and have heated the ring quickly. However, it is likely that as a beginner getting used to soldering you will have probably heated the ring for longer than strictly necessary and the metal may look quite dirty. Pickle in either dilute sulphuric acid (10:1) or safety pickle or boil in a solution of alum until the silver looks clean.

12. *Shaping*

The next stage is to make the ring round. Using the steel triblet, push the silver ring on as far as it will go (Fig 16). Using a rawhide mallet, hit the ring to make it round. You might want to lean the triblet against the workbench. It is important to use a rawhide mallet as it will not mark the silver (Fig 17). Turn the ring around and hit it again, this prevents the ring from becoming conical. If you find you have made the ring too small you can at this stage make it bigger. Hit the edge of the ring pushing it down the triblet, this stretches the ring. You may have to anneal the ring again if you need to stretch it very much.

13. *Cleaning up*

It is really important to hand finish the ring as perfectly as you can. Begin by filing off any excess solder (Fig 18). The quality of the final polish is entirely dependent on how well the ring is finished at this stage. For this project silicon carbide paper and Garriflex are all you need. Start by rubbing down the

depend on gravity so place the solder in the easiest place. In this case it is easier to balance the ring on top of the solder. Place the ring with the join directly on top of a pallion of solder onto the firebrick (Fig 14). With capillary action soldering it is important that all of the metal reaches the same temperature so heat the whole ring, not just the join area, aim the hot point of the flame at

Fig 16 Push the ring onto the mandrel as far as you can.

Fig 17 Tap the ring with the rawhide mallet.

Fig 18 File off any excess solder.

RIGHT: Fig 19 Pull down the edge of the ring.
FAR RIGHT: Fig 20 Rub down the inside of the ring.

edges of the ring by putting a sheet of silicon carbide paper (400) on a flat surface and rubbing the ring on its edge (Fig 19). Turn the ring over and do the other edge. Tear pieces of silicon carbide paper into small pieces and rub down the surface inside and outside the ring (Fig 20) or use a split pin attachment for the pendant drill. Keep changing the direction that you are working in so that the tiny scratches created by the silicon carbide paper keep crossing and recrossing. When the whole surface looks as even as possible you can move on to the Garriflex (Fig 21). Again work over the whole surface of the ring inside and outside, constantly changing direction. Now is a good time to check for firestain. Using the piece of tracing paper lay it on the surface of the ring, if you can see some darker areas that look grey under the tracing paper this is firestain. Use the Garriflex to remove the firestain (Fig 22). Now move on to the finer silicon carbide paper (1000) and again work over the whole surface in lots of different directions.

14. *Polishing*

First wash the ring in a mixture of ammonia, washing-up liquid and hot water using a wash brush or a soft toothbrush. This ensures that no gritty bits of silicon carbide or Garriflex transfer to the polishing mops to scratch the work. Then using Tripoli, polish the ring on the inside and outside. This can be done by hand if you do not have a polishing motor, it just takes longer. Ideally use a calico pendant drill mop to polish the inside and a calico mop on a polishing machine for the outside. Keep the mop well loaded with the Tripoli and use a firm pressure on the mop. As with the hand finishing keep changing the direction in which you are polishing. Tripoli is a very abrasive compound so be careful

Fig 21 Rub the ring with Garriflex.

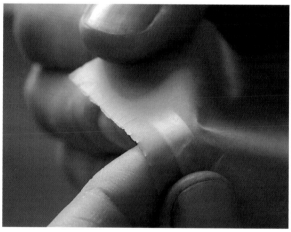

takes a bit longer. The impregnated silver polishing cloths that are available in most supermarkets can be used.

Practise these basic skills by making several rings varying the design. Try the following suggestions, before bending round into a ring shape (and always remember to anneal again if you have work-hardened the metal). By changing the edge of the ring, it does not have to be straight. Practise sawing a wavy edge. Saw shapes into the middle of the ring (*see* Fitting a Saw Blade), or saw decorative elements to solder on to the ring. Try changing the surface (*see* Chapter 5 Simple Decorative Processes). Try making several in different sections, using square wire and filing patterns into it, make several in different sized round wire to be worn together (*see* Chapter 5 Drawing Wire Down).

TOP LEFT: Fig 22 Use Garriflex to remove firestain.
BOTTOM LEFT: Fig 23 Check for firestain by looking at the surface of the silver through tracing paper.

POLISHING TIPS

◆ Keep separate mops for Tripoli and rouge and keep them clean and dust free.

◆ Always wash between the different stages with ammonia and soapy water. If you imagine what would happen if you were sanding down a piece of wood with coarse sandpaper and left bits of the sand on the surface and then changed to a finer paper, the coarser sand would scratch the surface and the same thing applies here. To get a really good polish you must make sure that at each stage the coarser abrasive has been completely removed before you move on to the finer one.

◆ A machine polish is only as good as the hand-polishing preparation allows it to be. There are no short-cuts here other than trying to prevent the metal getting badly marked in the first place. In fact, it sometimes takes as long to polish a piece as it does to make it.

SAFETY

◆ Tripoli and rouge dust as with any fine dust is hazardous to the respiratory system and eyes. Wear a mask and goggles when polishing.

◆ Ammonia is an irritant and the fumes can affect the eyes, skin and respiratory system. Use in a well-ventilated area.

that you do not polish away the edges. After you have finished with it, wash the ring and your hands in the ammonia and soapy water to remove any of the compound so that you cannot transfer it to the rouge mops. Go through the same process with the rouge, using swansdown mops, but with much less pressure. Wipe the ring through the edge of the mop, still changing direction. Finally wash in the ammonia and soapy water again to remove any rouge left on the ring, rinse in hot water and dry either in jeweller's sawdust, with a hair dryer or with a clean soft cloth.

If you have not got a polishing motor it is possible to polish by hand – it just

5 FURTHER TECHNIQUES

Once you have completed the basic processes covered in Chapter 4 you can start to incorporate some of the decorative techniques into your work. This chapter explains simple ways to texture the surface of metal. How to incorporate stones and mechanical fixings suitable for attaching materials that cannot be soldered. How to change the thickness and section of wire and an introduction to some of the textile techniques that can be used for jewellery.

SIMPLE DECORATIVE PROCESSES

Texturing

Texturing the surface of metal can provide interesting contrasts and add a sense of depth to the design particularly if combined with some of the different methods of finishing described in Chapter 6.

Hammered Texture

Using the different ends of hammers will produce different effects. A sharp-edged hammer will produce a bark effect and a ball-ended hammer a dimpled one. A planishing hammer makes a pattern of small flat circles, particularly if hammered over a slightly curved surface. Try collecting old hammers from car boot sales, and by filing, drilling and carving the ends you can make your own individual textures.

Matting punches are produced commercially and have a textured surface at one end to be hammered into the surface of the metal or you can make your own from steel stock by using files and drills or burrs in the pendant drill.

You can also use found materials, nail-heads, the edges of screws, meshes and other textures that you can hammer into metal to create texture.

Etching

Etching is a process where metal is removed by exposure to acid. This can be used as a decorative process on its own or to make a tool to print a design onto another piece of metal. To create a pattern on the surface of the metal an acid resist needs to be applied to some areas leaving the acid to attack other exposed areas. Interesting random textures can be made by using petroleum jelly, grease or wax crayons but these will be unpredictable. If you want a more precise result then etching varnish is much more controlled. Either paint the design on with the varnish or cover the metal completely and scratch the design away when it is dry.

For this technique you will need:
- Metal for etching
- Garriflex or Scotchbrite
- Acid-resist tape (or strong sticky-backed plastic or you can use the etcher's varnish on the back as well)
- Etcher's varnish
- A paintbrush
- A sharp scribe (or etcher's needle or sewing needle in a pin vice)
- A container for the acid (glass casserole dishes with lids are good but do not use for cooking and etching!)
- Acid
- A large feather (feathers are one of the few things unaffected by acid)
- White spirit and some rag

OPPOSITE PAGE:
Pendant copper/silver scent column. Loom woven and fabricated. Arline Fisch.

Earrings. Etched as a sheet then sawn out. Oxidized. Sarah Macrae, 1988.

GOLD	Although you can etch gold with 1 part nitric acid to 3 parts hydrochloric acid (this is known as aqua regia), it is a waste of an expensive material. Etching a piece of brass and roller printing the gold gives a similar effect without the potential for expensive mistakes and without any loss of gold
SILVER	1 part nitric acid to 3 parts water (this is a faster etch but tends to undercut the lines) *or* 1 part ferric nitrate to 4 parts water (much slower but much more accurate)
COPPER BRASS	1 part nitric acid to 1 part water *or* 1 part ferric chloride to 4 parts water

SAFETY

◆ When using acids take great care to assemble everything you need and think out what you are going to do.

◆ Wear protective clothing, rubber gloves, goggles and a respirator and work in a well-ventilated area.

◆ If you are splashed with acid, irrigate with large amounts of water.

◆ When mixing acids *always* add acid to water never the other way round. Acid and water do not mix easily and if you add water to acid, heat is generated and it will provoke a violent reaction. When pouring acid out of bottles, after the lid has been put back on, always rinse the outside of the bottle in case there are any drips of acid on the outside of the bottle.

◆ Bicarbonate of soda neutralizes acid and it is wise to have some in case of spills.

◆ Store acids carefully, make sure they are always accurately labelled and kept at a low level but secure and out of reach of children.

◆ Dispose of used acid carefully, do not pour down the drain, neutralize with bicarbonate of soda and pour onto the ground.

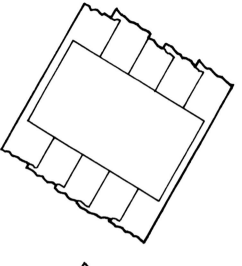

Fig 1 Cover the back with acid resist-tape leaving an overlap of about 1cm.

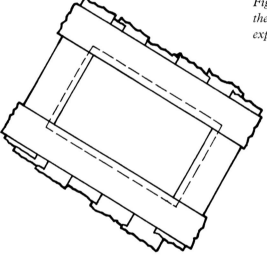

Fig 2 Put more tape on the front leaving an exposed area of metal.

◆ Ammonia and soapy water mix if ferric nitrate or ferric chloride are used.

Etching Silver with Nitric Acid

1. Slightly roughen the surface with medium Garriflex or Scotchbrite so that the varnish has a good surface to adhere to.

2. Degrease the metal well by scrubbing with a soft brush and ammonia and soapy water. Try not to touch the surface after you have cleaned it.

3. Cover the back with acid-resist tape leaving an overlap of about 1cm (Fig 1).

4. On the front face use the tape to make a border, again overlapping by about 1cm, sticking tape to tape thereby sealing the edges (Fig 2). This will save the edges of the metal from being eaten away.

5. Paint the remaining exposed area of metal with etching varnish. Try to get the covering as even as you can, thick enough that it looks black not brown but not too thick. Leave to dry somewhere warm for about an hour (Fig 3).

6. When it is dry (no longer sticky) use a sharp scribe (or etcher's needle or a

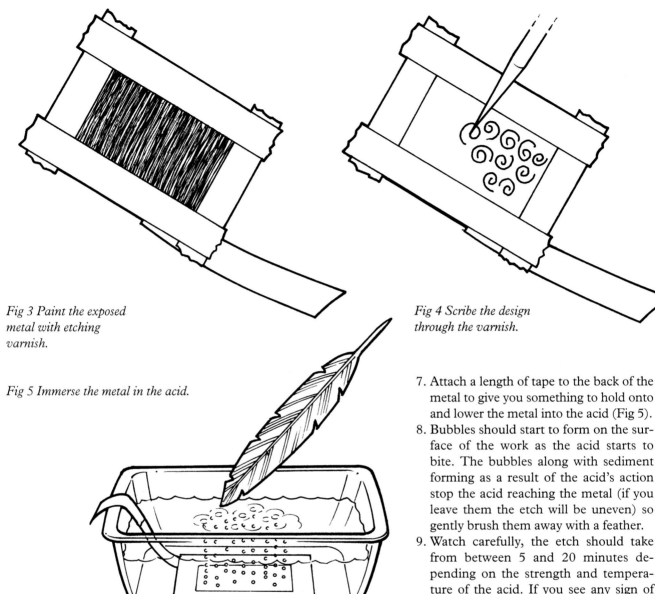

Fig 3 Paint the exposed
metal with etching
varnish.

Fig 4 Scribe the design
through the varnish.

Fig 5 Immerse the metal in the acid.

sewing needle in a pin vice) and scratch
the design through the varnish to the
metal underneath. Make sure that you
use sufficient pressure as if you scratch
too softly it can look as if you are
through to the metal but there can be
enough resist there to stop the acid
etching evenly (Fig 4).

7. Attach a length of tape to the back of the
metal to give you something to hold onto
and lower the metal into the acid (Fig 5).
8. Bubbles should start to form on the surface of the work as the acid starts to
bite. The bubbles along with sediment
forming as a result of the acid's action
stop the acid reaching the metal (if you
leave them the etch will be uneven) so
gently brush them away with a feather.
9. Watch carefully, the etch should take
from between 5 and 20 minutes depending on the strength and temperature of the acid. If you see any sign of
the varnish peeling off, remove the work
from the acid.
10. When the etching is as deep as you
want it to be, remove from the acid
and rinse in water thoroughly.
11. Peel off the tape and remove the varnish with white spirit and a cloth.

Nitric acid gives a faster etch (between 5
and 20 minutes) but tends to undercut.
Ferric nitrate and ferric chloride take

longer but will give a much more accurate etch. Because the etch takes longer (between one and four hours) it is impractical to stand with it, brushing away bubbles and sediment. To get around this, suspend the work face down in the acid. When the required depth of etch has been reached scrub well with ammonia, water alone will not stop ferric nitrate and ferric chloride. This form of etching is used to make circuit boards and some electronics suppliers sell a small etching tank that takes all the variables out of etching. It keeps the acid at a constant temperature, suspends the work in a wire cage and keeps the acid moving so that you should get perfect results every time, but at around £100 it is an expensive item unless you intend to use this technique a lot.

Photoetching
Photoetching is a technique where a design is transferred photographically using a light-sensitive resist. Several companies offer this service to jewellers and it is a cost-effective way for many studio jewellers to produce multiples.

USEFUL TIPS

It is useful to partially cover a scrap piece of metal with acid-resist tape and hang it in the acid at the same time so that you can check the depth of the etch without disturbing the resist on your work.

Try etching a length of tubing. Seal the ends with tape so that acid cannot leak inside the tubing then cover the tube with varnish. When it is dry, scratch a pattern into the surface and etch. After removing the varnish and tape, cut up into short lengths and use as beads.

If the work has been in the acid for a while and nothing has happened, try placing the acid container in a larger container of hot water.

Crown. Silver and gold plated brass. Photoetched, fabricated with cast settings. Sarah Tomlin, 1997.

Brooch. Silver and enamel. Photoetched. Jane Moore, 2000.

Roller Printing

This is a simple and very effective technique to create a textured surface to a sheet of metal. Fabric, paper, bandage, abrasive paper, paper doilies, lace, net, mesh and any similar materials can be used. Paper or thin metal foil can be cut into precise patterns or wire can be bent and shaped. Alternatively you can etch a pattern onto a sheet of brass and print it

Roller printing.

onto the metal. This can be a continuous pattern so that you have a sheet of pattern like a length of fabric that you can cut shapes out of afterwards. Think about the size of the shapes you are intending to cut out afterwards and make sure that the pattern is a suitable scale or you could end up without enough pattern on each piece. Or you could etch a specific design or even some writing (remember that the etching will need to be in mirror writing).

Roller printed ring with etched brass tools.

Earrings. Textured surfaces of silver and 18kt gold plated. Roller printed. EM Jewellery, 1998.

For this technique you will need:
- Metal to be printed. It is better to keep the size of the piece to about 50mm × 70mm or less as a larger piece becomes difficult to roll through the rolling mill.
- Printing material or etched brass sheet.
- Clean sheet of about 1mm thick brass the same size or larger than the metal to be printed.
- Rolling mill.

1. Anneal and pickle the metal to be printed. Make sure the surface of the metal is clean.

2. Place the printing material onto the silver with a protective sheet of brass on top, like a sandwich.

3. Open the rollers and close down onto the 'sandwich' of metal and printing material. Winding the handle of the rollers towards you, remove the sandwich from the mill. The rollers are now set to the thickness of the sandwich.

4. Close the rollers down by about half a turn. The amount you need to close the rollers varies depending on the size of the piece to be milled. The pressure needs to be enough that it is difficult to turn the handle but not so tight that it takes two people to do it.

Brooch. Silver, 18kt gold and garnet. Roller printed with paper. Georgina Taylor, 1985.

Brooch. Silver, 18kt gold and opal. Roller printed with paper. Georgina Taylor.

Reticulation
Also known as *Samorodok*
(Russian for 'born by itself')

Reticulation is a technique for giving an organic skin-like texture to the surface of standard silver by using a controlled melting of the surface. Initially you will find it is difficult to control and the results are largely accidental, but with practice it can be controlled. There are some beautiful examples of this technique to be seen among Russian silverware. Start with a piece of silver slightly larger than you need and between 10g and 16g thick depending on how large a piece you want to use. It will be difficult to reticulate, for instance, a 10cm square piece of 10g without melting holes into it, however a small piece will be fine.

Reticulation works on standard silver through raising a pure silver layer on the surface that melts at a slightly higher temperature than the standard silver underneath. As the metal is heated and the core of standard silver melts, it expands and then rapidly cools and contracts as the flame is moved further along the metal, wrinkling the pure silver on the surface.

Preparing the Silver
Anneal the silver with an oxidizing flame (a blue flame without any yellow showing) and then quench. Pickle and then scrub with a brass brush and pumice (or Scotch-brite and pumice).

Repeat this at least four times (ten is better) until the surface of the silver stays white when it is heated. This is the pure silver layer forming on the top of the standard.

Reticulating
Heat to annealing temperature and then using a small hot flame concentrating the heat in one area and moving along to the next as reticulation occurs. Be ready to pull the torch away as soon as you see the effect you want. The air from the torch, particularly if you are using a torch with compressed air, tends to push the silver into waves, so experiment with the angle and the distance of the torch from the surface.

Localizing the reticulation
If you want to localize the reticulation leaving part of the metal smooth then coat the area to be left with coolheat paste. This seems to be very effective in stopping any reticulation where it covers the surface but allows the silver to be reticulated right up to the edge of the paste.

MECHANICAL METHODS OF FIXING

There are several ways in which pieces can be put together without using solder. The advantages of using mechanical methods of joining bits together are that you can

Rings. 9kt gold wire with 18kt gold-plated edges. Reticulated silver with gold plating. EM Jewellery, 1997.

completely finish all of the elements of the piece before you assemble them. It is worth considering a mechanical method if the design means that it is going to be difficult to polish or if you want elements to be hard and springy and soldering is going to anneal them. Incorporating and combining other materials with metal means you have to consider mechanical methods of connecting and enclosing. Traditionally, incorporating another material usually meant setting a stone but can also include how to attach a piece of slate or acrylic to metal or how to contain feathers or fabric. To start with the basic way of setting a stone. The principle of setting is to contain the stone in enough metal to secure it but not enough to obscure it. The most important consideration is how you solve the practical problem of retaining the stone or other material while still working with the aesthetic of the piece. In other words the whole design should work together so that it looks right.

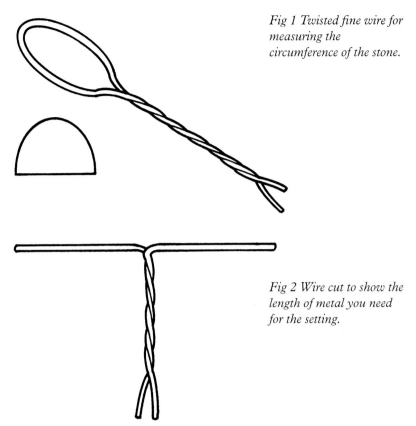

Fig 1 Twisted fine wire for measuring the circumference of the stone.

Fig 2 Wire cut to show the length of metal you need for the setting.

Basic Collar Setting for a Round Cabochon Stone

1. Begin by measuring the circumference of the stone. The easiest way to do this is to use a piece of fine wire (binding wire will suffice). Make a loop around something of a similar size (small triblet if you have one), and twist the ends together (Fig 1).

2. Fit this loop over the stone and adjust until the loop fits the stone. Cut through the loop and straighten out. This will give you the length of the strip of metal you need to cut (Fig 2).

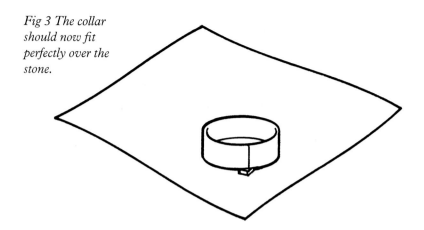

Fig 3 The collar should now fit perfectly over the stone.

Fig 4 Various heights of settings.

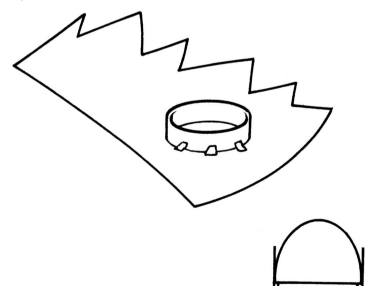

Fig 5 The setting soldered onto a flat sheet.

3. Then make the setting in exactly the same way that you made the band ring. If you can put the setting over the stone and pick it up you know you have a perfect fit (Fig 3).

The height of the setting will depend on the curve of the stone and also where the setting is to be used (Fig 4). If the setting has to be soldered onto a flat sheet and the stone has a flat base then solder the setting onto the sheet and it is ready to set after cleaning and polishing (Fig 5). If the setting is to be soldered to a curved surface or the stone has not got a flat base or if you want the setting to have an open back then it needs to have an inner bezel or ring (Fig 6). This is another ring soldered inside the setting for the stone to sit on. You can buy shaped bearer wire for settings but it is just as easy to make an inner bezel. Use a small amount of binding wire to secure the inner bezel in the right place and solder it into the setting (Fig 7), placing the solder on the bottom of the setting (Fig 8). File the bottom of the setting so that it will fit where it is intended to. If it is to be soldered to a ring the setting needs to have a curve. Solder the setting to the piece. File the top edge of the setting until there is just enough metal to turn over and hold the stone.

Setting the Stone

Once the setting has been made and soldered into position, clean up and polish the whole piece. Setting the stone should be the last job to do. Make sure that the

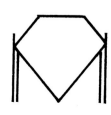

Fig 6 The setting with an inner bezel.

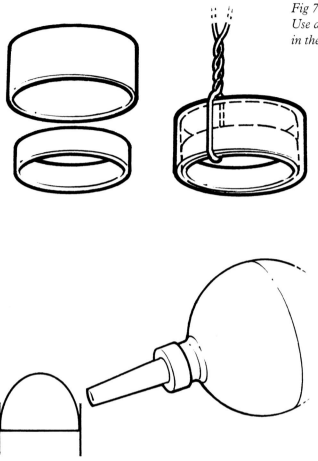

Fig 7 Make a bezel to fit just inside the setting. Use a small amount of binding wire to secure it in the right place and solder it into the setting.

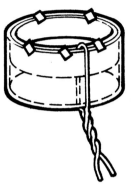

Fig 8 Place the setting upside down and put the solder on the bottom of the setting.

Fig 9 Support the work either in a ring vice or against the bench peg. Firm pressure is needed to push the metal over. It may need to be filed slightly thinner if it will not push over.

Collection of four 18kt gold, sapphire and iolite rings. Jeanne Werge-Hartley.

stone is sitting down straight in the setting. Find a position at your workbench where you can support the setting against the bench peg, or use a wooden ring clamp (Fig 9). Most jewellers customize their bench pegs and you may find it helpful to file a small curve into the bench peg to push the setting against. Using a setting pusher, firmly push the metal over the stone at four points (Fig 10). Then push over the four points in between (Fig 11). Continue in between the eight points until the metal has been pushed over all round the stone. At this point put your finger over the top of the stone and see if it wobbles in the setting. If it does not, then you have pushed the metal over tightly

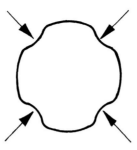

Fig 10 Using a setting pusher, firmly push the metal over the stone at four points.

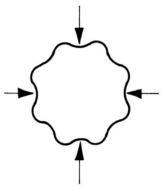

Fig 11 Then push over the four points in between.

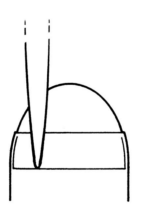

Fig 12 Stroke around the setting with the burnisher with as much firm pressure as you can, smoothing the metal.

enough. If it moves only slightly then the next stage of burnishing around the setting may be enough to tighten it. Stroke around the setting with the burnisher with as much firm pressure as you can while smoothing the metal (Fig 12). Finally give the piece a gentle buff with rouge. If the stone is very soft, however, protect it from the mop with your thumbnail.

USEFUL TIPS

If the stone is still moving slightly after burnishing, try polishing the edge of the setting with a hard felt mop. The action of pushing the setting against a felt mop will tighten the setting further.

If the setting has an enclosed back it is a good idea to drill a small hole in the back before you try the stone in the setting so that if it gets stuck you can use a piece of wire to push it out. Or alternatively an effective but not completely foolproof way is to use a small piece of Blu-Tack to pull the stone out of the setting.

If you need to file round a setting use a barrette or safety back file to minimize the risk of damage to the surrounding area. It is also sensible to cover all vulnerable areas with masking tape.

BELOW: Fig 13 The top edge of the setting does not need to be straight but can be filed and shaped.

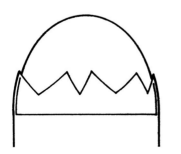
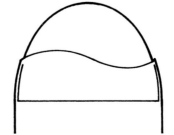
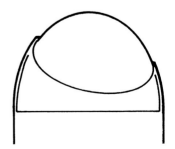

Variations

For an oval stone make the setting round and then squash slightly with your fingers if it is big enough or with parallel pliers, leaving the solder join on the long edge (if you have the solder join on one end it will be more pointed than the other).

The top edge of the setting does not need to be straight but can be filed and shaped (Fig 13).

Claw Setting

Claw settings (Fig 14) are the logical development from collar settings in that more and more metal is taken away from around the stone until you have the minimum required to hold the stone in place. Traditional coronet settings are produced commercially and if you want to use this sort, it is easier to buy one. However, there are many other ways to set with claws that are more interesting. The claws do not have to be evenly spaced and regular or even all the same size, and as long as the metal can be pushed over the stone in some way then the stone is set. Look at the design of the piece and use the decorative elements of the design to set the stone. Or if you are starting with the stone look at the lines, shapes and patterns in the stone to help you design the piece, maybe interpreting the lines as wires that could hold the stone in place. There are some very specialized types of setting such as channel setting and pavé but they require specialized skills and are not relevant to someone just starting.

Setting from the Back

Sometimes the solution is to set the stone from behind, perhaps because the decoration is going to be damaged by setting or because you want to keep the front very plain (Fig 15).

Setting can be used to fix other materials as well as the more obvious semi-precious and precious stones and it depends on your idea as to whether these are suitable methods.

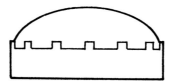

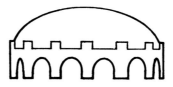

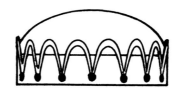

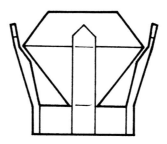

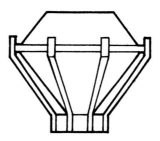

Fig 14 Variations of simple claw settings.

Fig 15 Setting a stone from behind. Decoration soldered to the top of the setting needs to be shaped so the stone fits comfortably behind it. File tabs on the bottom of the setting and make an inner bezel (this need only be wire). When you are ready to set the stone push the inner bezel up behind the stone and turn the tabs over to secure it.

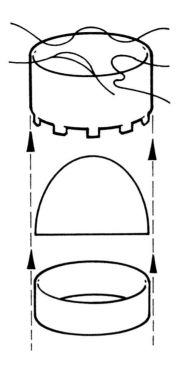

Fig 16 Fit the wire of the rivet through the holes in the materials to be joined.

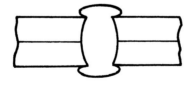

Fig 17 When tapped with a hammer on both ends the rivet compresses along its length and secures the pieces together.

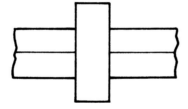

Fig 18 Riveting two pieces of metal with another material between. Drill the holes in the materials to be joined making the hole in the non-metal parts very slightly larger so that the action of compressing the rivet does not split the material.

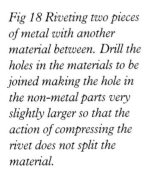

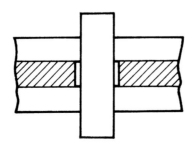

Riveting

Materials like slate, acrylic or wood are all soft enough to be drilled so riveting them in place is one way of securing them. If you are going to have metal either side of the other material then a solid rivet will be fine. A solid rivet is basically a short length of wire, fitting tightly through holes drilled in the materials to be joined, that when compressed along its length secures the pieces together.

It is helpful if you match the wire to the drill size so that you know the rivet will fit the hole. If you do not have quite the right sized drill then use one smaller than you need and gradually make it bigger with a round file. It is vital that the wire fits tightly in the hole for if it is loose the rivet will not hold.

1. Cut a short length of straight and annealed wire and file one end flat at the end (square).
2. Drill the holes in the materials to be joined making the hole in the non-metal parts very slightly larger so that the action of compressing the rivet does not split the material.
3. Fit the wire through the holes. Push the wire through so that it is protruding by slightly less than the width of the wire. File off the other end leaving the same amount protruding (Fig 16).
4. Place one end of the rivet on a steel block and tap the other end with a small hammer two or three times (Fig 17). Turn over and tap the other end of the rivet in the same way. Repeat until secure.

If the material is fragile and using a hammer will risk damaging it then a tube rivet would be better (Fig 19), either a simple tube or a tube with a fixed end (Fig 20). A fixed end can be an unobtrusive disc or dome or can be a decorative shape or even a stone setting. With this type of rivet there is no need to use a hammer. Put the sharp point of a scribe into the end of the tube and wind

Earrings. Silver,
tortoiseshell and 18kt
yellow gold. Bo Davies.

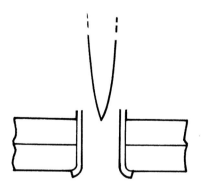

Fig 19 A simple tube rivet.

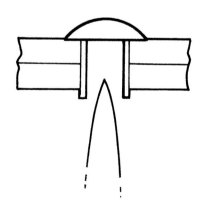

Fig 20 A tube rivet with a fixed end.

round at an angle until the tubing opens out and holds the material in place.

For a moving rivet, for example if you want to be able to turn part of the piece, rivet the pieces together with a cardboard washer in between and then soak out the cardboard. The rivet will still be secure but it will allow the pieces to move. Another way of securing delicate pieces is to use wires soldered to the back of the metal pieces that then pass through holes drilled in the non-metal material. The wires are then spiralled and burnished down.

To make a piece of wire straight either put one end in a vice and pull until you feel the silver stretch slightly and then twist, or if it is a short length roll it between two heavy pieces of steel.

USING WIRE

Wire can be drawn through drawplates to change the size and the section of the wire. Wire can be woven, knotted, knitted, plaited, twisted or wrapped, in fact just about every textile technique using thread can be translated into metal. Fine wire can make incredibly flexible fabric that jewellers can and do use in many different ways. Wire can also be used to construct forms, it can be forged, bent, hammered and rolled. It can also be curled and soldered to sheet as surface decoration.

Annealing Wire

It is important to anneal wire evenly. If unevenly annealed then it will break at the harder points when you try to use it. The best way to anneal wire is in a kiln but this is not usually very practical unless you are wanting to anneal a large amount. To anneal wire with a torch, coil the wire and bind it with a small amount of binding wire so that there are no stray bits of wire that can overheat. Use a soft reducing flame and keep the flame moving. Watch carefully to see that all of the wire gets to dull red heat and none gets too hot. An alternative method is to make a steel box and fill with charcoal chips. Heat the steel box to red heat with the wire inside so that the wire is heated by the heat diffusing through the steel rather than direct heat from the torch.

Changing Thickness and the Section of the Wire

When using wire in a piece of jewellery it is important to think about the section of the wire and use something appropriate to your idea. If the feel of the idea is very machine-like with crisp straight lines and sharp angles it may be appropriate to use square section to emphasize the mechanistic aesthetic. Alternatively, if the piece is very delicate in feel, but needs the wire to provide structural strength, then it might be useful to use a rectangular section with the thinner edge visible to the front and the thicker edge providing the strength. Forging the wire by placing it on a steel block and using a hammer to make it thicker in places and thinner in others makes the line that the wire makes more lively visually.

The same is true of drawing; the most exciting drawings to look at have variation in the weight of the line.

Part of a silver necklace incorporating woven chain. Sarah Macrae, 1989.

Drawing Wire Down

To change the thickness or the section of the wire a drawplate is used. Cut a length of wire and file a point starting about 15mm from the end. Anneal the wire (it is important to anneal after you have filed the point as filing hardens the point and it will snap off when you try to pull the wire through the drawplate). Secure the drawplate in a vice or draw bench. Run a piece of beeswax or soap down the length of the wire and put the point through the drawplate in the hole nearest to the original size of the wire. Using draw tongs or parallel pliers apply a steady pull, pulling the wire through the hole. Repeat through the next hole and so on until you have pulled the wire to the size you want. The wire will need annealing again after four or five holes or possibly less with thick wire. It is always better to anneal more often than not as the wire will start to 'peel' if it is too hard. Wire up to about 2mm thick can be pulled down by hand using the drawplate in a vice but for wire of a greater thickness you will need to use a draw bench.

Using the Rolling Mill

Rolling mills usually have a section for square wire and sometimes for half round that can be used for changing round to square or half round or for making square wire smaller or tapered (*see* page 135). The flat rollers can also be used to roll square wire rectangular and round wire oval.

Soldering Fine Wires to Sheet

Soldering a fine wire to a sheet of metal can cause problems due to the difference in the volume of the two pieces. To get the two pieces to the same temperature so that the solder flows and joins them together is often a major problem for beginners. What generally happens is that the wire heats up much quicker than the sheet and either it melts before the sheet has reached soldering temperature or the solder jumps onto the wire and stubbornly refuses to flow

Drawing wire down.

between the wire and the sheet. If the wire is intended to be attached flat onto the sheet, it can be held in place either with steel cotter pins (that you can buy) or with titanium clips (*see* Chapter 4). The main advantage with using titanium is that it is physically impossible to solder it to the work. It is also better to heat the work from underneath at least to start with, aiming at getting the sheet hot first. Steel mesh is excellent for supporting the work allowing the flame to be directed underneath. If it is intended that the wire only be attached to the sheet in places, the cotter pins/titanium clips are often the easiest way to hold the wire in place – however the vulnerable bits are where the wire is not in contact with the sheet. This is where a heat sink is needed. A heat sink can be anything that draws the heat away from the wire to stop it rapidly getting to melting point – for example, a pair of steel tweezers (or spring tongs) just touching the wire, or a length of binding wire either leaning against it or wrapped round it. There are various types of paste or gel that are produced commercially as heat sinks or even a small lump of clay out of the garden works well. Positioning the piece so that the fine wires are in contact with the firebrick is another alternative.

GOLD WIRE TIP

If you are pulling gold wire down, solder a short length of silver wire to the end to pull through the drawplate so you do not mangle the end of the gold wire with the draw tongs.

TEXTILE TECHNIQUES

Traditionally the way to make a flexible fabric from metal was chain mail. When made with small links at jewellery scale this feels beautiful to wear. Silver lace has also been used extensively historically for military uniforms and court dresses. More recently almost any textile technique using yarn has also been applied to wire. Knitting, French knitting, crochet, macramé, bobbin lace making, tatting, kumi himo braiding and weaving are just some of the possible techniques that can and have been used.

Silver wire must be well annealed and for some techniques has to be annealed during the process. Higher karat gold wires work well as does coloured copper electrical wire. Practise the technique with yarn first. It is probably sensible to learn to

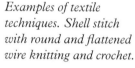

Examples of textile techniques. Shell stitch with round and flattened wire knitting and crochet.

knit with wool first and then transfer the skill to the wire.

The main difference between yarn and wire is that if you make a mistake in the wire it is usually very difficult, if not impossible, to undo. The wire will break either while trying to undo or when trying to redo the stitch or knot.

Woven Chain

This is a very simple way of making a chain from a single length of wire. The technique is basically French knitting without the cotton reel. It can be done with any number of loops but it is easier to start with just three.

1. Begin with a length of about 60cm of annealed fine wire (about 0.5mm or finer). A longer length tends to get kinked

Chain mail. The relationship between the thickness of the wire used and the size of the links can vary depending on whether a tight compact chain mail or a looser more open effect is required. The links can be all the same size for a very even machined feel, or they can vary in size and shape. Small shapes can be incorporated and again these can be all the same, or they can be all different shapes.

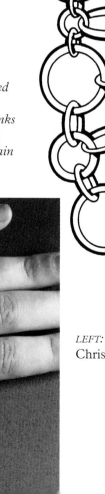

LEFT: *Chain mail hand ornament.*
Chrissie Savage, 1990.

RIGHT: *Fig 1 Make three loops leaving about 5cm spare at one end.*

BOTTOM RIGHT: *Fig 2 With the short end (5cm) bind the loops together in the middle.*

Necklace. Knitted silver.
Anna Keen.

and work-hardened and this way it is easier to join new lengths on as you need them.

2. Make three loops leaving about 5cm spare at one end (Fig 1).
3. With the short end (5cm) bind the loops together in the middle (Fig 2).
4. Adjust the loops so they are an even trefoil shape.
5. Pass the long end up through the first loop and out through the second loop (Fig 3).
6. Using a scribe to control the size of the loop, pull the loop tight on the scribe and tip the loop up towards the middle slightly. If you are making a very fine chain use the wrong end of a drill or a darning needle

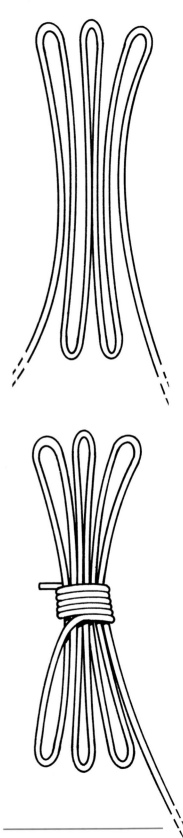

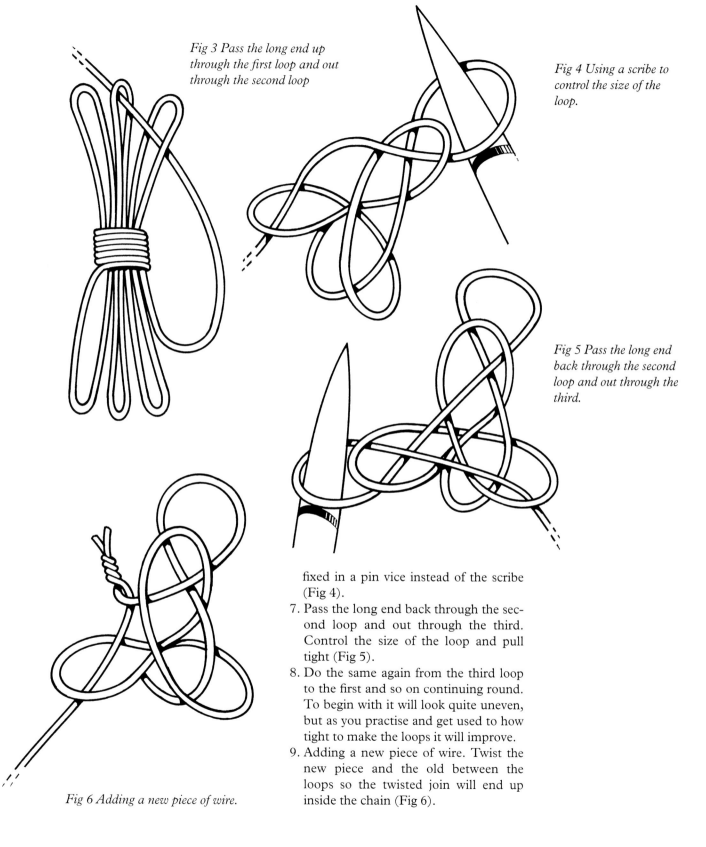

Fig 3 Pass the long end up through the first loop and out through the second loop

Fig 4 Using a scribe to control the size of the loop.

Fig 5 Pass the long end back through the second loop and out through the third.

Fig 6 Adding a new piece of wire.

fixed in a pin vice instead of the scribe (Fig 4).

7. Pass the long end back through the second loop and out through the third. Control the size of the loop and pull tight (Fig 5).

8. Do the same again from the third loop to the first and so on continuing round. To begin with it will look quite uneven, but as you practise and get used to how tight to make the loops it will improve.

9. Adding a new piece of wire. Twist the new piece and the old between the loops so the twisted join will end up inside the chain (Fig 6).

*Necklace. Silver and
anodized titanium chain
mail with lapis lazuli.*
Michael Pinder, 1982.

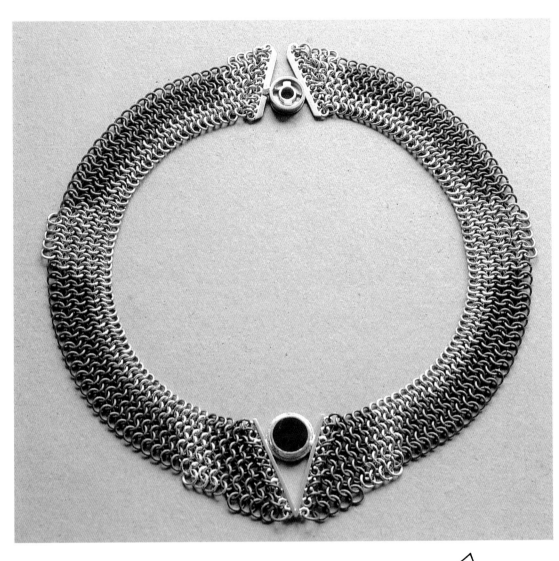

10. When you have woven the length you want, pull it through a drawplate to even it up.
11. To make the chain more flexible clamp a length of wooden dowelling into a vice and wrap the chain round it once. Pull backwards and forwards vigorously (Fig 7).

Shell Stitch

This is a very free form of wire work in that it grows in whichever direction you decide – the shells do not have to have the same number of stitches or be the same

Fig 7 Making the chain more flexible.

Necklace, 'Copper Cascade'. Coated copper, fine silver, machine knit, crochet edges. Arline Fisch, 2000.

size unless you choose them to be. This stitch works well with a flattened wire.

1. Begin with a length of about 60cm of annealed fine wire (about 0.5mm or finer). A longer length tends to get kinked and work-hardened and this way it is easier to join new lengths on as you need them.
2. Make two loops and bring the long length up between them (Fig 8).
3. Loop the long length into the first loop from the back to the front (Fig 9).

Fig 8 Make two loops and bring the long length up between them.

Fig 9 Loop the long length into the first loop from the back to the front.

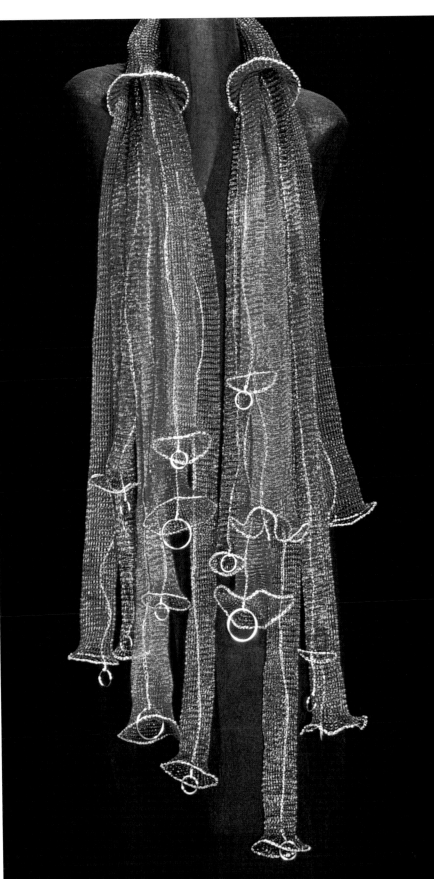

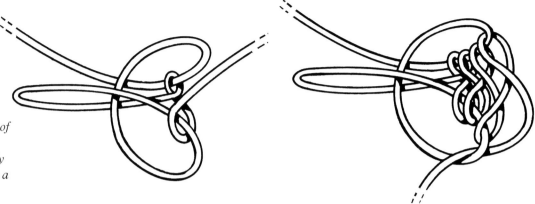

RIGHT: Fig 10 Loop the long length through the second loop from back to front.

FAR RIGHT: Fig 11 Keep weaving the wire from one loop to the other in a figure of eight shape making each figure-of-eight shape slightly bigger until you have made a shell shape.

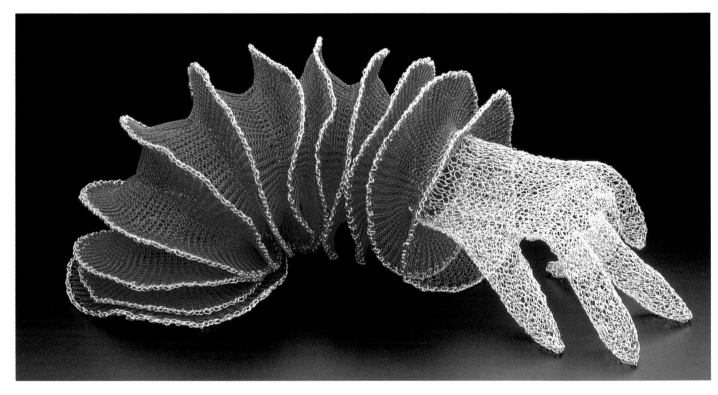

Arm ornament. 'Bracelet and Glove'. Coated copper, fine silver, machine and hand knit. Arline Fisch, 1999.

4. Loop the long length through the second loop from back to front (Fig 10).
5. Keep weaving the wire from one loop to the other in a figure-of-eight shape making each figure-of-eight shape slightly bigger until you have made a shell shape (Fig 11).
6. To make the next shell, work between the last figure-of-eight loop of the last shell and one of the original loops (Fig 12).
7. Keep adding more shell forms allowing each to grow out of the last one (Fig 13).
8. To join more wire on, leave a 5–10cm tail and start a new shell form between two others. It should be tight enough at the base of the shell to hold. When the area of shell stitch is finished, weave the tail's ends into the back.

Cosmos Brooch. Knitted copper wire, garnet gems, glass and brass beads. Jan Truman, 1994.

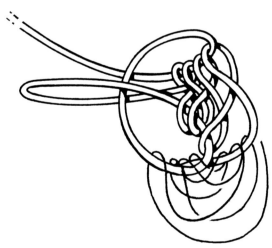

Fig 12 To make the next shell, work between the last figure of eight loop of the last shell and one of the original loops.

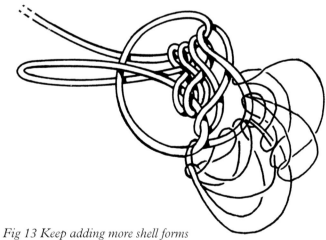

Fig 13 Keep adding more shell forms allowing each to grow out of the last one.

PROJECT 3

WIRE EARRINGS

Materials

- An old wire coat hanger
- 70mm of 1mm wire
- 120mm of 0.9mm silver wire (ear wires)
- Medium solder
- 3,600mm of 0.5mm silver or copper-coated wire
- Borax or FM solution

Tools

- Ring triblet
- Saw and 3/0 saw blades
- Needle files
- Soldering equipment
- Bench vice
- Punch or dowelling
- Pliers (round, flat, snipe)
- Shears
- Polishing equipment or silver polishing cloth
- Ammonia and soapy water and a soft brush

1. Anneal the 70mm of 1mm wire and wind round the end of a steel punch or the small end of the ring triblet to make a spiral about 10mm in diameter (Fig 1). Saw through to make two links (Fig 2).

2. Make a loop from wire cut from an old coat hanger, clamp the ends in a bench vice and bend towards you so that you have a sturdy fixed loop to which to attach the fine wires (Fig 3).

3. If you are using silver, anneal the fine 0.5mm wire. Make sure you coil the wire tightly so that there is less chance of over-heating (Fig 4).

4. Cut the 0.5mm wire into twelve lengths (six for each earring) using shears and fold each length in half.

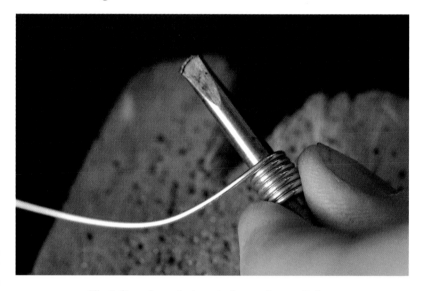

Fig 1 Wind the wire round the end of a steel punch.

BELOW LEFT: *Fig 2 Saw through the spiral to make two links.*
BELOW RIGHT: *Fig 3 A loop made from wire from an old coathanger.*

Fig 4 Anneal the silver wire.

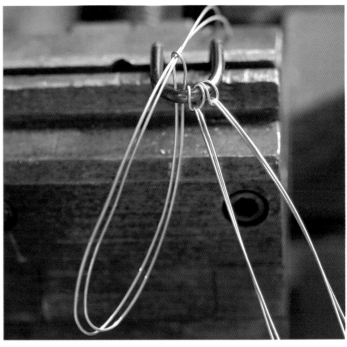

Fig 5 Attach each length to the loop, which is fixed in a vice.

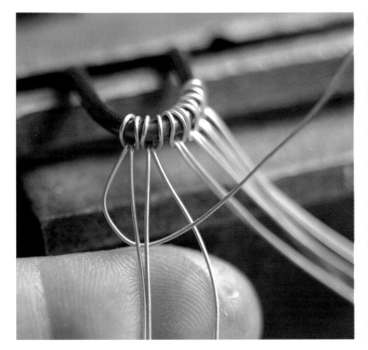

Fig 6 To start a flat knot, pass the wire on the left under the middle two and over the wire on the right.

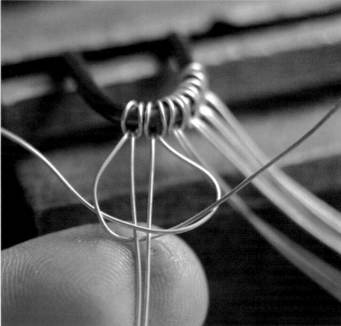

Fig 7 Pass the wire on the right over the two in the middle and through the loop made by the wire on the left.

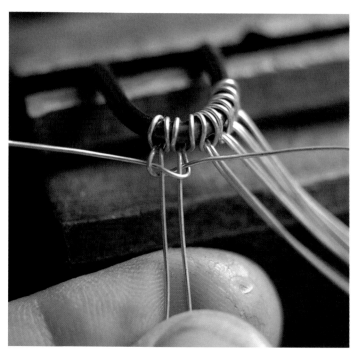

Fig 8 First half of the flat knot.

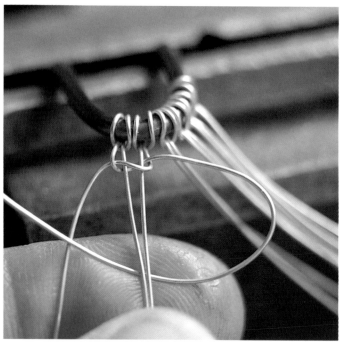

Fig 9 Pass the wire on the right under the two in the middle and over the wire on the left.

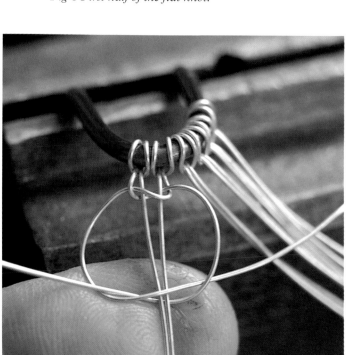

Fig 10 Take the wire on the left over the two in the middle and through the loop made by the wire on the right.

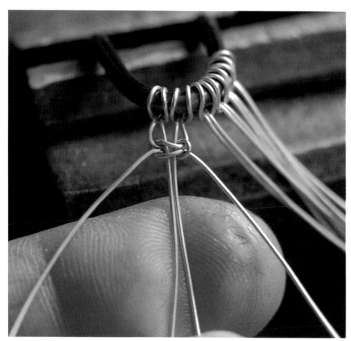

Fig 11 The completed flat knot.

Fig 12

Fig 13

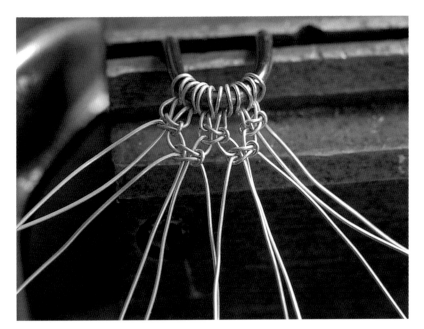

Fig 14

5. Pass the loop end of each double wire through the loop of the coat hanger wire, pass the free ends through itself and pull tight. Attach all 6 wires to the loop in this way (Fig 5).

6. Divide the wires into 3 groups of 4 wires and tie 3 flat knots (Figs 6–12).

7. Divide the wires into 2 groups of 4 leaving out 2 wires at either end (Figs 13 and 14). Tie 2 flat knots.

8. For the next row use the same wires as in the first row but allow the wires to fan out slightly.

9. If you are using silver wire it will need annealing half-way through. Coil the wire up and bind with twisted binding wire and anneal carefully (Fig 15).

10. Repeat 7 and 8 down the length of the wire (Figs 16 & 17).

11. Repeat for the second earring looking carefully at the first earring as you tie each knot endeavouring to make them as similar as possible. Alternatively make 2 loops out of the coat hanger wire and work both earrings at the same time.

12. When you have finished tying all the knots, using the point of a scribe, gently even out the loops between the knots to even out the pattern (Fig 18).

Fig 15 Annealing.

13. Slide the earrings off the coat hanger wire.
14. Trim the free ends with shears and scroll up into spirals using round-ended pliers (Figs 19 & 20).
15. Open out sideways the two links (Fig 21) you made at the beginning and slide the earring on, and close the link (Fig 22).

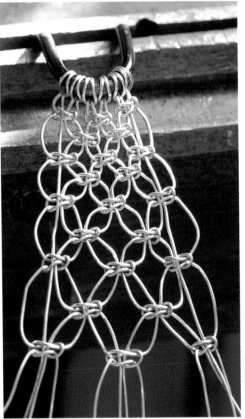

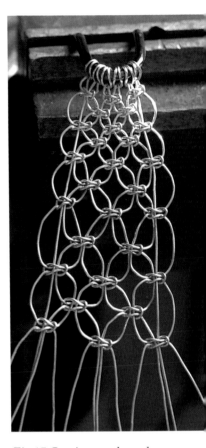

Fig 16 Repeat points 7 and 8 to the end of the wire.
BELOW LEFT: Fig 18 Use the point of a scribe to even out the loops.

Fig 17 Continue to the end of the wire.
BELOW: Fig 19 Scroll the ends of the wires.

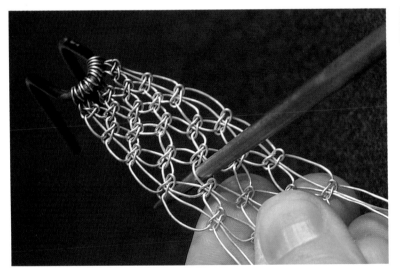

ABOVE: Fig 20 Slide the earring off the coathanger wire loop.

TOP RIGHT: Fig 21 Open two links sideways.

MIDDLE RIGHT: Fig 22 Slide the earring onto the link and close it.

RIGHT: Fig 23 Make a loop at the end of the wire.

16. Make ear hooks out of the 0.9mm wire. Curl the end with round-nosed pliers to make a loop (Fig 23), then using your fingers curve the wire to make a loop to go through the ear (Figs 24 & 25). Open the small loop by twisting sideways (Fig 26), put the ring at the top of the earring into the small open loop in the ear wire and close by twisting it back straight again (Fig 27).

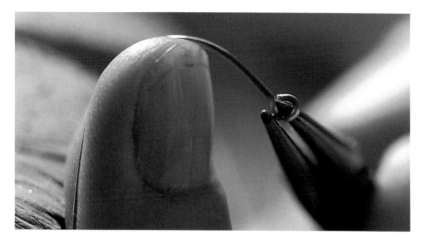

LEFT: *Fig 24 Use your fingers to curve the wire into a hook.*
BELOW LEFT: *Fig 25 Put a slight bend at the end of the wire.*

BELOW: *Fig 26 Open the loop sideways.*
BOTTOM: *Fig 27 Pass the large link at the top of the earring through the loop on the ear wire and close the loop.*

Finished earrings in silver and in copper
On the finished earrings in the photograph (*see* page 108), I have made a spiral first before making the loop on the ear wire to bring an element of the earring design into the ear wire shape.

As with the first two projects try making several pairs of earrings in different lengths, metals and colours; try mixing the copper and silver or using different thicknesses of wire; try using more wires or less to make different shapes.

6 FASTENINGS, FINDINGS AND FINISHING

Before the invention of buttons, poppers and zips, a piece of jewellery often had a quite specific function to hold pieces of clothing together. Some of these ancient fastenings have a very satisfying completeness of decorative form and function. The fibula and penannular brooches in particular were used extensively by people of many cultures and they vary from the elaborately decorated to the simple and functional. Some of the Celtic penannular brooches found in Ireland had a ceremonial function as well and are very large – some around 40cm in length – and

as they are worn with the pin pointing up toward the shoulder they could evidently be quite dangerous. It was written into the ancient laws of Ireland that each individual was responsible for any damage caused to anyone else by the pin of his penannular. The penannular also occurs in other cultures, notably amongst North African tribesmen although where the Celts tended to decorate the circle the North Africans decorate the end of the pin.

Findings refer to the units that make the piece of jewellery function. This includes ear wires, brooch fastenings, and necklace

OPPOSITE PAGE:
Penannular brooch (reversible). 18kt gold with diamonds and opals on one side, tourmaline, peridot and diamond on the other. Sarah Macrae, 1994

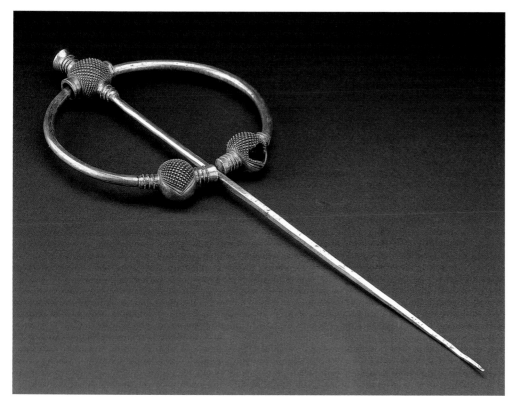

Newbiggin Moor silver 'Thistle' brooch. © The British Museum.

or bracelet clasps. Ideally in my opinion the way the piece works should be integral to the form of the piece. It should be conceived as part of the form, not just 'stuck on' as an afterthought purely to attach the piece to the wearer. In other words try to consider the type and style of the fastening to ensure that it is appropriate to your idea. Look at the basic principle of the finding and then adapt and develop it so that it suits your work. The examples illustrated in this

in the jewellery manufacturing trade, the fastening can sometimes take longer than the rest of the piece. Although the examples here are simple they need to be made well, the lines and shapes must be good and this often takes some practice. Even the simplest fastening can look like a nasty bit of bent wire if the shapes are not good.

Finally this chapter looks at finishing. The finish on a piece of jewellery can really make or break the final result. In the end

Fibula brooch. Sarah Macrae, 2001.

chapter are some of the simplest to make technically. There are many more advanced types of fastening that take considerably more time and skill to make but for a beginner it is better to keep the findings simple so that you progress faster making a series of pieces that allow you to develop your ideas while also handling the materials and practising the basic skills of making. In highly technically sophisticated pieces, particularly

any surface will change with wear and time whether it is a highly polished or a textured surface, for example, by being constantly rubbed. There are many ways of treating the surface, some of which are covered here. The only way to ensure that you retain the surface you want is to protect it with raised decoration or a surrounding protective wire so that the surface is not touched during normal wear.

BROOCH FASTENINGS

Fibula

The oldest type of brooch, the fibula, is formed from a single piece of metal in the same way as a simple safety pin. The metal is forged to shape and hardened so that it is springy and can be curled round one end to make the catch. The other end is sharpened to make the pin and curled round at least twice to allow the pin to spring into the catch.

The Penannular

This is also an ancient form of fastening and penannular means literally broken circle. It works by having a pin with a tube or hole at the end of it. A broken circle of wire passes through the tube or hole that should be a loose enough fit so that the circle moves freely. Move the circle to the front out of the way of the pin and push the pin through some fabric. Then turn the circle under the pin and this will lock it into place. Penannular brooches occur in many cultures but the Celts are perhaps the best known ancient culture to use them. Many ancient Celtic penannular brooches are very ornate and richly decorated with chip carving (a sort of very deep engraving) and with stones and some are very plain and simple, but invariably they chose to decorate the circle rather than the end of the pin. African brooches, however, generally focus on the end of the pin and the circle becomes smaller and less significant. Double penannular brooches are also worn with two brooches joined by decorative chains from the end of the pins.

Separate Pin

The brooch pin does not have to be attached to the brooch. The pin can be straight, curved or even wiggly as long as it can be either pushed through the work and the fabric or through loops and fabric.

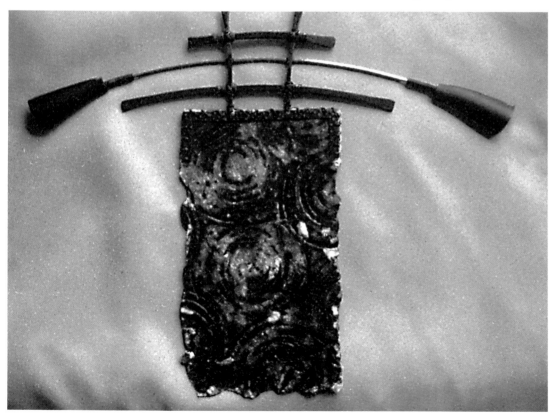

Recycled paper brooch with a separate pin. One end of the pin can be removed to pass the pin through the fabric. Elizabeth Haynes.

Simple Pin and Catch

You need:
A piece of wire between 1–2mm thick and about 60mm plus the length of the pin (at least 25mm) long.

Cut the length of wire and slightly flatten the first 5mm of each end with a hammer on a steel plate (Fig 1). Bend the flattened 5mm of wire at right angles to the rest. Solder flattened ends down to the back of the brooch (Fig 2).

Fig 1 Flatten the ends of the wire.

Fig 2 Attach the wire to the back of the brooch. Cut the wire where shown.

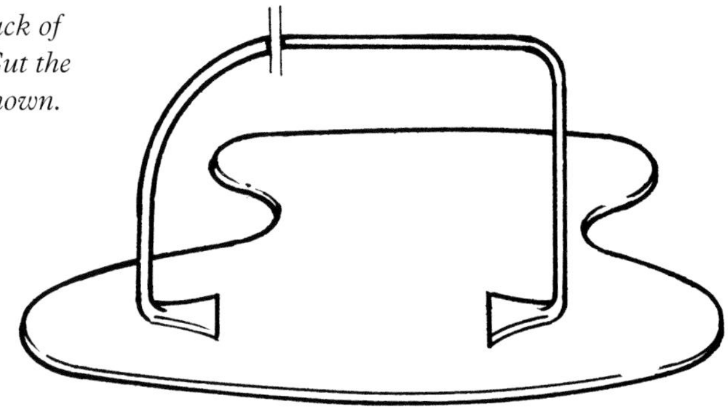

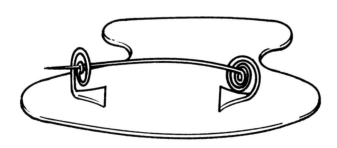

Fig 3 The finished pin and catch.

Clean up and polish the brooch. Cut the loop about 20mm from one end (which end depends on whether the brooch pin is going to run vertical or horizontal – if vertical the short length should be at the bottom, if horizontal the short length should be on the left, looking at the back of the brooch. Using flat pliers pull the two pieces of wire and twist to harden them. With round-nose pliers curl the short length to make the catch and curl the longer end three times round the wrong end of a needle file to make a spring and file the end to a point (Fig 3).

ALTERNATIVES. To make this pin neater at the back instead of flattening both ends of the wire, feed them into holes drilled to fit the wire and solder in.

Double Pin

You need:
A length of wire twice the intended length of the catch plus 10mm. The wire should be between 1–2mm thick.
   Approximately 10mm of tubing. The diameter of the tubing will depend on the thickness of the wire but it should be a tight fit.
   A strip of 10g sheet 25–35 mm long by 3mm wide.

Cut a piece of wire and anneal. To straighten and harden the wire, put one end in a vice and with a pair of parallel pliers pull the end of the wire and twist about one and a half turns, you should just feel the wire start to stretch when pulling hard enough. File the ends of the wire to points.
   Cut approximately 10mm of tubing, file a small flat edge along the tube to stop it rolling when you need to solder it.
   Cut the strip of 10g sheet and file. Mark the centre point and make a right angle bend 5mm either side.
   Solder the tubing and the centre part of the strip to the back of the brooch (Fig 4).

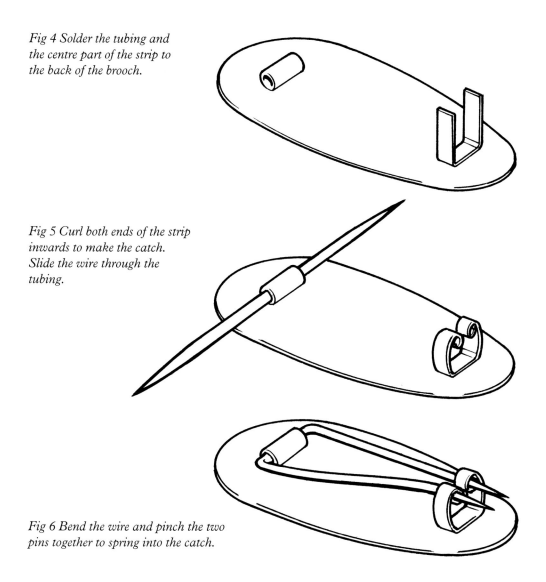

Fig 4 Solder the tubing and the centre part of the strip to the back of the brooch.

Fig 5 Curl both ends of the strip inwards to make the catch. Slide the wire through the tubing.

Fig 6 Bend the wire and pinch the two pins together to spring into the catch.

After all cleaning up, finishing and polishing, curl both ends of the strip inwards towards each other to make the catch (Fig 5). Finally slide the wire through the tubing and making sure that the wire is an even length both sides, bend the wire at slightly less than right angles to the tubing. You should have to pinch the two pins together to spring into the catch (Fig 6).

NECKLACE FASTENINGS

Fish Hook

The simplest form of fastening. Start with a length of wire somewhere between 0.5mm and 2.0mm thick. The exact thickness depends on the scale and weight of the necklace, but anything thinner than 0.5mm will not be strong enough in silver and thicker than 2.0mm will look clumsy

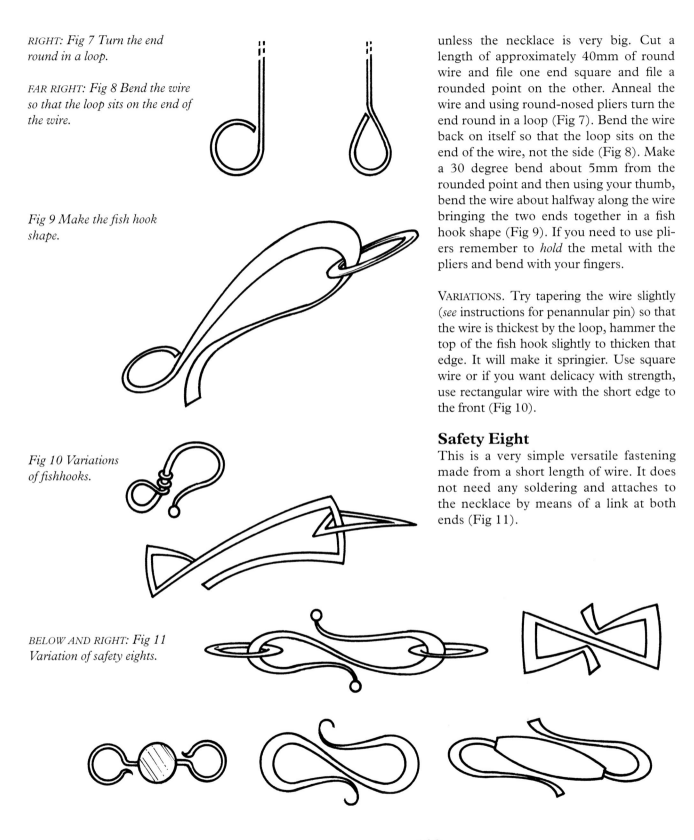

RIGHT: *Fig 7 Turn the end round in a loop.*

FAR RIGHT: *Fig 8 Bend the wire so that the loop sits on the end of the wire.*

Fig 9 Make the fish hook shape.

Fig 10 Variations of fishhooks.

BELOW AND RIGHT: *Fig 11 Variation of safety eights.*

unless the necklace is very big. Cut a length of approximately 40mm of round wire and file one end square and file a rounded point on the other. Anneal the wire and using round-nosed pliers turn the end round in a loop (Fig 7). Bend the wire back on itself so that the loop sits on the end of the wire, not the side (Fig 8). Make a 30 degree bend about 5mm from the rounded point and then using your thumb, bend the wire about halfway along the wire bringing the two ends together in a fish hook shape (Fig 9). If you need to use pliers remember to *hold* the metal with the pliers and bend with your fingers.

VARIATIONS. Try tapering the wire slightly (*see* instructions for penannular pin) so that the wire is thickest by the loop, hammer the top of the fish hook slightly to thicken that edge. It will make it springier. Use square wire or if you want delicacy with strength, use rectangular wire with the short edge to the front (Fig 10).

Safety Eight

This is a very simple versatile fastening made from a short length of wire. It does not need any soldering and attaches to the necklace by means of a link at both ends (Fig 11).

Cut approximately 70mm length of round wire. Similar to the fish hook, it needs to be around 0.5mm to 2.0mm thick depending on what is going to look right with the piece. It is better to err on the side of making it too thick rather than too thin. File both ends of the wire into a rounded point and then anneal. Bend the wire in thirds with your fingers, use pliers to hold the wire if necessary; bending with pliers will mark it.

Then just tip the last 5mm of wire either end at a 30 degree angle.

VARIATIONS. Solder a decorative element to the centre of the wire before you bend it. Taper the wire slightly at the ends and hammer to spread wire at the curves to get a flowing feel of thick to thin. Use different section wire. The shape can be angular rather than rounded.

Detail of necklace. Roller printed silver, ebony inlay, and 9kt gold. Each section is reversible and joined with a safety eight so that the necklace can be worn in different ways. Sarah Macrae, 1994.

Necklace. Silver carved acrylic and rock crystal beads. Sarah Macrae, 2000.

Necklace with three positions in silver with 24kt plate. Photoetched and hollow constructed with bayonet clasp. Shelby Fitzpatrick, 1998.

Bar and Link

Take a short length of wire and either bend a loop halfway along it or solder a loop on. Attach a short length of chain (half the length of the bar) to the loop. For the other end make a link that the bar and chain can pass through. From this basic fastening there could be variations. The bar does not have to be straight, the link does not have to be round, the wire can be different sections. The bar can have interesting terminals. The loop can be decorated round the edge or can be a hole in a larger area of decoration.

BELOW: Detail of fastening of feather necklace. Sarah Macrae.

BOTTOM: Bar and link variations.

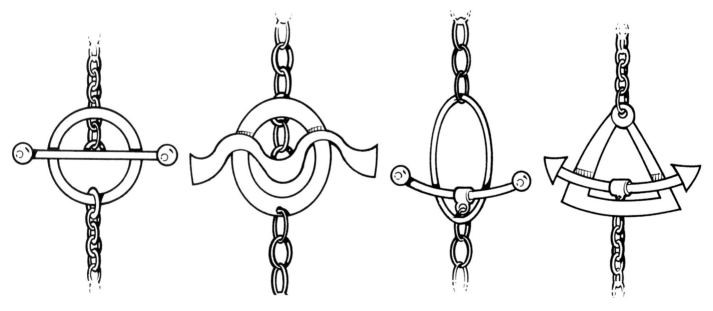

MEASURING TIP

If you are in any doubt about the amount of wire to cut, you can either measure by making up the hook in binding wire or, if you have a drawing, work the binding wire to the drawing. Then straighten out the wire and measure it.

Or start with a coil of silver wire, make the hook on the end and then cut and file the rounded point end.

Earrings. Roller printed silver, ebony inlay, and 9kt gold.
Sarah Macrae, 1994.

Ear Wires

As with other findings it helps to think about the overall design of the piece so that the ear wires become part of the whole design. Ear wires are usually made of 0.9mm thick wire that fits comfortably through the ear.

For instructions on how to make basic ear wires *see* Project 3.

To make ear wires with a shape at the top that reflects the design of the earrings, cut 60mm of 0.9mm wire for each earring.

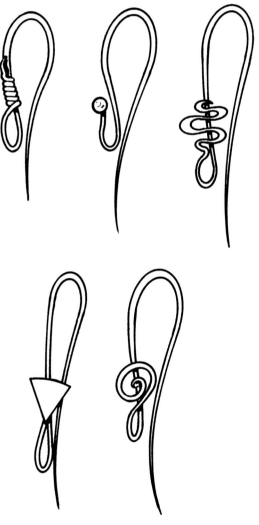

Ear wire variations.

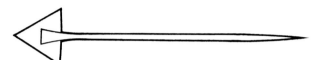

LEFT: *Fig 1 Solder the ear wire to a shape that reflects the earring.*

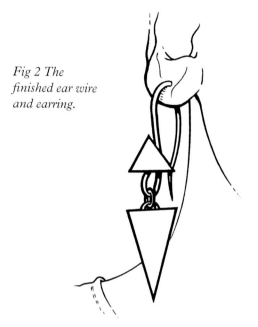

Fig 2 The finished ear wire and earring.

Flatten one end slightly to allow a good surface area for soldering. Cut out a suitable shape that reflects the earring and solder the ear wire to it (Fig 1).

Clean up and polish. If the ear wire seems soft and not springy enough, hold both ends in pliers and pull and twist one to two times to harden the wire. Bend the loop to hold the earring with pliers and the loop to go through the ear with your fingers. The earring will not come off the ear wire because of the soldered shape at one end and the ear at the other (Fig 2).

ALTERNATIVE METHODS OF FINISHING

All over machine polishes can look very uninteresting. If the whole surface is highly reflective the form of the piece can be lost. There are lots of different ways of treating the surface, or try combining different

Pendant. Silver, 18kt gold and opal matrix. Silver finished with Scotchbrite and the gold burnished. Helen Clifford Jones, 2000.

Rings. Oxidized silver and gold with peridot, garnet and tourmaline. Ute Sanne, 1988.

finishes. Think about what kind of surface is most appropriate to your idea.

Burnishing

Before the development of abrasives and sophisticated polishing equipment, jewellers used burnishing to finish the surface. It has many advantages, no metal is removed, it needs very little equipment, it work-hardens the surface of the metal and there is substantially less risk of ruining the piece at the last minute after many hours of work. As a surface it has a subtlety that highly machine-polished surfaces lack. Burnishing is a technique in which a harder substance is rubbed against a softer one to smooth it. Other disciplines such as ceramics and printmaking also use burnishing. Ancient jewellers often used polished agate and you can still buy agate burnishers. More usually, jewellers use polished steel burnishers and these come in a wide range of shapes and sizes. It is important to keep burnishers highly polished and to protect them from getting badly scratched.

Garriflex

The finest Garriflex (brown) gives a good satin finish and it is very useful if you want to combine a polished and satin surface. Highly polish the surface first and then mask out the areas you want to stay polished with masking tape. It is a good idea to burnish the edges of the masking tape down so that you get very crisp edges. Then rub over the exposed area with Garriflex either in circular movements or in a direction to produce the effect you prefer.

Peel off the masking tape, or soaking it off in hot water sometimes works better.

Oxidizing

Oxidizing with Liver of Sulphur gives silver a range of colours from yellow through blue and purple to dark grey depending on the strength of the solution. Sulphur is usually bought in lump form and has a fairly short shelf-life (about six months if kept in an airtight container). It is also sometimes available in liquid form that lasts much longer. For method, *see* Project 4. The usual method is to oxidize the whole piece after polishing, then to repolish with rouge to remove the oxide from the high points giving a greater sense of depth to the piece. However, if you want a very localized area the solution can be painted on using a nylon or other man-made fibre paintbrush (sulphur will destroy any natural hair brush). Oxidizing copper works very effectively and turns the copper black. Silver oxidizes dark grey. If you want to colour silver as black as copper, you can copperplate the silver by putting it in some pickle (safety pickle or dilute sulphuric acid)

with some steel and then oxidize. This can be particularly effective if the piece is silver with gold decoration. Oxidizing the surface with sulphur and then burnishing gives a lovely steely grey surface almost like haematite. Household bleach will also colour silver a sepia brown to black.

Satin Finish

Scotchbrite and pumice
Scotchbrite (the green pan scourer more usually associated with washing-up) on its own gives a bright textured finish that is particularly useful for inaccessible areas like the inside of boxes, but it can also give a dramatic finish particularly if used in addition to burnished or polished areas. It is made in several different grades, green is fairly coarse and brown is fine. You can buy Scotchbrite mops to fit on polishers. If the Scotchbrite is used in combination with pumice powder it gives a very soft satin finish. To use pumice with a Scotchbrite mop, mix the pumice to a paste with a small amount of olive oil and then paint it onto the work, then present to the mop. Pumice is the abrasive in most household scourers.

Scratch or Burred Finish

This works best in small localized areas and is also useful for difficult-to-get-at areas. Experiment with different ways of scratching until you find an effect you like. Try using a very sharp scribe and make small circular movements until you have covered the area consistently. Cross-hatching also works as well as more random scribbling.

Penannular brooch (reversible). Silver and cloisonné enamel (both sides). Sarah Macrae, 1994.

Cloisonné enamel penannular brooch. Sarah Macrae, 1992.

Try using a sewing needle held in a pin vice. Dental burrs or phrasers in a pendant drill can also be effective but are less easy to control. If possible, protect other areas with several layers of masking tape.

NOTES ON FINISHING

Surface finishing is usually the last process in the making of a piece but if sections are to be connected mechanically – that is, screwed together or riveted, then they can be completely finished, protected with masking tape and then connected.

Sometimes the slower method is best if to do the thing quicker involves equipment that can do damage to your piece. A slip with a pendant drill can in seconds cause several hours' remedial work.

To achieve a really good satin finish the work should be finished to a good polish first and then taken back to satin.

Wire Wool
Wire wool is made in different grades of coarseness. The household pan scouring grade is fairly coarse but wire wool sold for finishing wood is very fine. As with the Scotchbrite a different surface is achieved with or without pumice. Make circular motions on the surface.

White Finish
The most consistent method of achieving a really good white finish on silver is to boil the piece in a solution of alum (aluminium potassium sulphate). Mix a tablespoon of alum with about a pint of water in an old enamel saucepan, add the piece you want to whiten and boil until the desired effect is achieved.

Penannular brooch.
Acrylic and silver in ebony
box. Sarah Macrae,
2000.

Penannular brooches.
Roller printed silver.
Sarah Macrae, 1998.

PROJECT 4

A SIMPLE PENANNULAR BROOCH IN SILVER

If you want to try this project do not feel you need to follow the shapes exactly, try and vary it and come up with your own shape. The only constant is the pin and the circle and even they can vary slightly. The pin can be straight or curved or even wiggly as long as it will pass through whatever fabric you intend pinning it to. The circle will still work as a locking device whatever shape it is as long as it will move through the tubing and has a gap for the pin.

Materials
- 110mm of 2mm wire (the circle and pin)
- 130mm of 1mm square wire (about 70mm for around the edge and 50mm for the curl and zigzag decoration)
- 4mm of 5mm tubing
- 30mm × 20mm of 14g sheet
- Medium solder
- Liver of Sulphur

Tools
- Pair of snips
- Bob drill
- 2mm drill stock
- Pliers (round, snipe and flat)
- Needle files
- All soldering equipment (torch, FM solution or borax, tweezers, paintbrush, firebricks, etc.)
- Ring mandrel
- Rawhide mallet
- Sawframe
- 3/0 sawblades
- Two steel blocks for flattening and hammering onto
- Small metal (small planishing) hammer
- Silicon carbide paper
- Garriflex
- Two clean jam jars
- Polishing equipment
- Ammonia and soapy water and a soft brush

1. Cut the 2mm wire into two pieces, one 50mm and one 60mm.

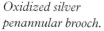

Oxidized silver penannular brooch.

The pin

2. Drill a 2mm hole in the side wall of the tubing and file a small flat on the opposite side, so that when you come to solder the tubing to the main shape of the brooch there is a bit more contact (Fig 1).

3. File the end of the 50mm length of 2mm wire flat (square) and insert into the 2mm hole in the tubing. This makes a much stronger join and also makes positioning it for soldering much easier. Only push the pin into the tube by the thickness of the tube wall, do not block the tubing.

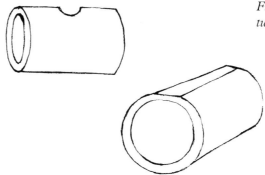

Fig 1 Prepare the tubing.

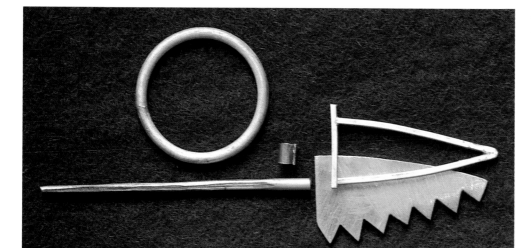

Fig 2 The prepared elements of the brooch.

The circle

4. Solder the 60mm piece of wire into a circle and make perfectly round on a ring mandrel with a rawhide mallet (Fig 2).

   Polish to harden up as much as possible. Saw through the join and stretch slightly on the mandrel so that there is a gap of about 3–4mm.

The decorative shape

5. Bend the 1mm square wire bend into shape for the decorative end of the brooch. Cut off the excess and file the ends so they fit together tightly. Solder together. Flatten between two pieces of steel so that it will lay flat on the piece of 14g sheet (Figs 3 & 4).

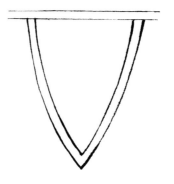

Fig 3 Bend the 1mm square wire into shape.

6. Cut a shape out of the 14g sheet slightly larger than your wire shape.

7. If you want to add any further decorative elements to the shape like the curl and zigzag in the example then make it

Fig 4 Flatten between two steel blocks.

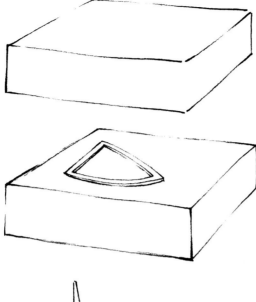

Fig 5 Sharp bends need to be filed before annealing, bending and soldering (see page 64).

section on making crisp bends). Pre-solder with as little solder as you can (that is, run the solder on the backs of the piece/s) first so that you do not get solder over the surface of the sheet (sulphur will not oxidize solder). Pickle if necessary (Fig 5).

8. Solder the tubing to the top of the shape and the pin to the tubing. Solder the wire shape and any decorative element down flat to the shape you have cut out of the sheet of 14g putting the pallions of solder around the outside of the wire shape where it will be easier to clean off any excess. If you can, set up and solder all in one go. The fewer times you heat the work, the less firestain will occur (Fig 6).

9. File the pin to a point. Another way is to feed the pin through the wire section of the rolling mill in stages to make a stepped taper first, then to hammer with a planishing hammer and then to file. The advantage to doing it this way is that you start with 30mm of wire and it stretches to 50mm and so is more economical. The disadvantage is that it takes a little more skill and practice (Fig 7).

10. Clean up with silicon carbide paper and Garriflex.

11. Polish (*see* Band Ring project).

12. Attach a length of wire or string to the tubing so that the whole brooch can be dangled in the sulphur.

13. Dissolve a small lump (marble-sized) of sulphur in half a jam jar of recently boiled (that is, very hot) water and have another container of very hot clean water. Dip the brooch into the clean water for a few seconds and then into

now. To make a curl, file the wire slightly thinner at the end that you intend to be nearest the middle, so that it will curl round tighter. Hold the filed end with round-nosed pliers and bend the wire round with your fingers. If you want crisp bends on the zigzag, the bends need to be filed and soldered (*see*

SAFETY

Sulphur fumes are unpleasant, use either in a fume cupboard or work outside standing upwind.

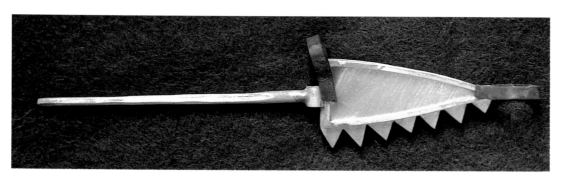

Fig 6 Solder the elements together.

the sulphur for a few seconds. Repeat until you have reached the depth of colour that you desire. The reason for only dipping for a few seconds at a time is that if the oxidized layer becomes too thick it tends to flake off.

14. Re-polish with rouge to remove the oxidizing from everywhere but the recesses.

15. Open the circle by twisting it sideways, slide one end through the tubing and twist again to close. Then with the brooch tipped up, hammer the open ends of the circle on a steel block with a small metal hammer so that the wire spreads to stop the circle being able to feed back through the tubing. re-polish the ends if necessary. The gap in the circle should be just wide enough for the pin to pass through (Fig 8).

16. If, as in the example, you wish to curve the pin gently, ease the pin into a curve.

For further security you can file a groove in the circle to locate the pin or solder two tiny balls to the circle to locate the pin, or you can curl up the flattened ends with pliers.

To wear a penannular brooch bring the circle forwards so it is out of the way of the pin, push the pin through a small amount of fabric. Move the circle back and turn it so that it goes under the pin and locks it in place.

Having understood the principle of how a penannular brooch works, now try making one where the circle is the decorative element instead of the end of the pin.

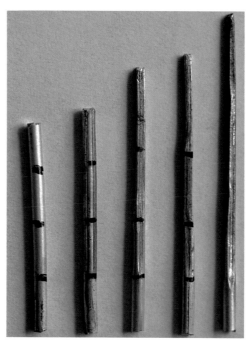

Fig 7 Using a rolling mill to make a taper.

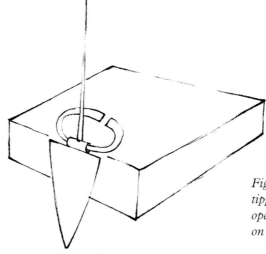

Fig 8 With the brooch tipped up, hammer the open ends of the circle on a steel block.

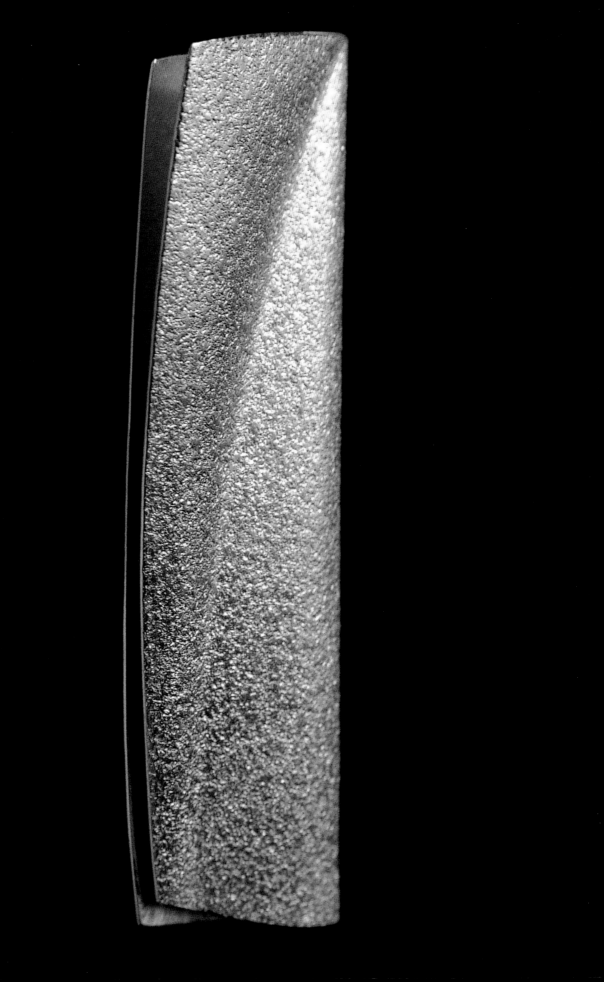

7 DEVELOPING YOUR OWN IDEAS

When starting to develop your own ideas it is important to realize that no designer sits down with a blank sheet of paper and somehow miraculously designs a piece. Design should be, and is, a personal voyage of discovery. As the educationalist Marion Richardson said of children's art 'Unless a child is expressing his own vision he is expressing nothing at all.'

We are all individuals with our own experiences and no two people, even when given the same brief and source material, will come up with the same solution. There is some evidence to support some people having a greater genetic predisposition to being creative, but motivation also plays a very large part. No-one would argue against the fact that learning to play a musical instrument competently involves concentrated and regular practice. At undergraduate level this involves many hours' practice every day. If you want to be a jeweller, even at amateur level, then the thinking, drawing and making skills need to be practised regularly. Everyone has some ability that can be nurtured and enhanced and it does help to know that there is a process and that the sudden flash of inspiration is more myth than reality. Occasionally an idea will seem to just come to you but not without the thinking, preparation and research going on as well. If you wait for inspiration to strike, you could wait forever. For a beginner there needs to be a period of investigation and research to develop a vocabulary of shapes, forms, patterns and textures that are personal to the individual alongside

practising the basic skills of making. Developing the design skills alongside the making skills is, I believe, much the best way of enabling your ideas to grow in complexity as your practical skills develop. This chapter offers a process that can help to form this vocabulary and help you to arrive at unique and individual ideas. It is based on the research of psychologists into creative thinking and there is a brief explanation of the thinking behind it.

CREATIVITY

The study of creativity and the creative process by psychologists is a relatively recent one. The first person to recognize that there was a process that could be identified was a French mathematician called Poincaré. In 1913 while working on a new mathematical theory he described the thinking that underpins every creative activity as:

- identifying the problem
- the research into it
- the period of uncertainty and maturation
- the flash of insight
- the rationalization

In 1926 a psychologist called Wallas refined this idea further and described the stages as:

- preparation
- incubation
- illumination
- verification

OPPOSITE PAGE:
Brooch. 18kt textured yellow gold, press formed. The subtle form of this piece has its origins in drawings of the human figure. Jacqueline Mina.

This sequence of events makes more sense for design students translated as:

- research
- development
- realization
- analysis

Research

Research consists in investigating possible starting points, seeking and collecting source material, looking, drawing and thinking. If you are a student working to a brief then your research may be specific and prescribed or if you are a maker working for a client then the work and therefore the research may have externally applied limits and boundaries. If you are free of external restrictions then the research can be as wide-ranging or as narrow and specific as you choose.

Development

Development is taking the source material and starting to do something with it. As the designer you are a kind of filter, everything you see and experience goes in and comes out again coloured by your individuality. This is the most difficult stage to understand and to learn. This stage can and often is a struggle and is as much about confidence and conviction as it is about 'talent'. It is having to make choices (is that line right, is that space too big, are the proportions all right) and in the end the only person who can make those decisions is you, although a good teacher can help you. This stage often involves drawing the ideas many times, making small adjustments each time until it seems to be right.

Realization

The making of the piece, the realization of the idea.

Analysis

In some ways this is the most important stage of the process and often the stage that gets forgotten and missed out. When the piece has been finally made, has it worked the way you wanted it to, how would you do it differently if you were to make it again, does it express what you wanted it to? This analysis should inform the next piece of work and the next and so on, so that the work moves forward each time. It is very rare for makers to be totally satisfied with a piece; there is, and should be, a constant dialogue going on with the work to refine and improve.

This process is not a linear one with each stage being completed before moving to the next, but fluid. A maker will move in and out of the different stages as the idea progresses. The making often starts before the development is complete and the piece will change and develop further during the making. Analysis should be going on throughout, all the time you are making choices about what to look at, what to draw, which shapes to develop. You might start with research or you may start with the bare bones of an idea that you then need to research around.

THEORIES OF CREATIVITY

There are two main theories as to what constitutes creativity. There is the Stimulus–Response theory that was first written about by a psychologist called Medrick in 1962. He defined creativity as making associations between stimuli and responses that are characterized by the fact that the elements linked together are not normally associated. Divergent or creative-thinking people tend to link stimuli with highly individual responses. The game show 'Blankety–Blank' relies on the most uncreative response to a given stimulus, in other words the response most commonly given by most people.

Cognitive theory is about the way we organize all the information that our senses are bombarded with all our waking hours.

Bruner in 1957 suggested that we have to filter all this information to avoid what he referred to as cognitive strain. We do this by relating all new information to previous experience and then mentally filing it. We do not normally look at each experience as isolated and unique. Bruner called this data-coding. For example when you enter a room and observe a chair you do not have to rediscover what a chair is, you see it, your brain relates it to previous experience and recognizes that it fits into the category of things to sit on. You do not waste mental effort in thinking about it, you just sit on it. Life would certainly be exhausting if each and every experience was perceived as being unique. However, to be creative according to Rogers you need to be open to experience and to be aware of the unique qualities of each experience. This involves being observant and really seeing and noticing things around us.

Millennium necklace. Gold collar set with tourmalines and diamonds inspired by the sea and the Christian symbol of the fish. Each fish represents a different decorative style which has personal significance to the maker from the last 2000 years. Jeanne Werge-Hartley, 2000.

*Firebird brooch
based on the ballet
by Stravinsky.*
Jeanne Werge-
Hartley, 1998.

There are lots of ways to encourage creative thinking. Brainstorming is an activity where from a starting point (this might be a word, an image or an idea) you write down anything and everything that occurs to you. This is usually done with a group of people and the fundamental rule is that nothing is discounted, criticized or excluded during the brainstorm. If you cannot persuade friends or family to join in then you can brainstorm on your own. Afterwards the resulting mass of words can be sifted and pruned. Word association can help (try using *Roget's Thesaurus*) as can image association, too. Think of your starting point – what does it bring to your mind visually? This may throw up some very illogical associations but that does not matter. The point is to keep your mind open to all sorts of possibilities.

Keeping a sketchbook as a visual diary is another aid to creative thinking. Get into the habit of carrying a small sketchbook with you everywhere so that you can make a note of a shape, a colour, a texture or anything else that you find interesting. The sketchbook does not need to be just for drawing; you can stick things in it, or simply write a note to remind you of something.

So to summarize these ideas about creativity, creativity is:
- the ability to make highly individual associations
- to have flexible mental categories
- to be open to experience
- to be observant.

WAYS OF BEGINNING TO RESEARCH

Spidergram

When thinking about gathering source material you might like to start by brainstorming all the things that interest *you*. Begin by making what is called a 'spidergram' of everything and anything in your life which is important to you or that you find visually exciting. Put down everything, however irrelevant it seems – artists or makers that you find inspiring, interests and hobbies you are involved in, anything that you collect or do that makes you an individual. It helps to do this over several days, pin up some paper somewhere visi-

Research

When you feel you have written down all you can, look at the different areas on the spidergram and choose one to research further. The next stage is to visually research this area. Depending on what is appropriate you could collect images (postcards, photocopies, images cut from newspapers or journals) or you could make drawings or take photographs or all three. While you are doing this think about why you are choosing the images, what is it that appeals to you. Gather as much visual information as you can. You might choose to organize all these images into a sketchbook or a folder or if you have a working area you may choose to pin them up around you.

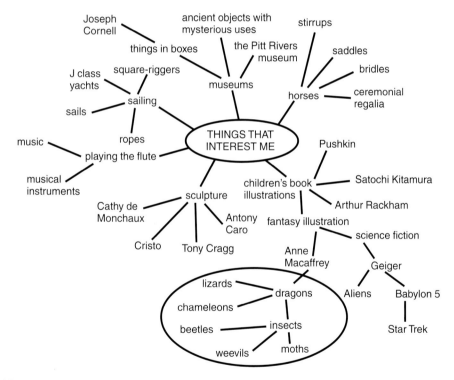

Spidergram of the author's interests.

ble (near the kettle is often a good place) and keep adding to the spidergram as things occur to you. Sometimes it also helps to do this with someone else.

In the example of a spidergram above, an area has been selected (within the oval line), which could then be researched further by collecting images out of magazines, photocopies from biology books, illustrations from children's books, drawings of dead (or alive!) insects, illustrations of

Collecting source material.
Student design area with
accumulated material to
inspire and inform.

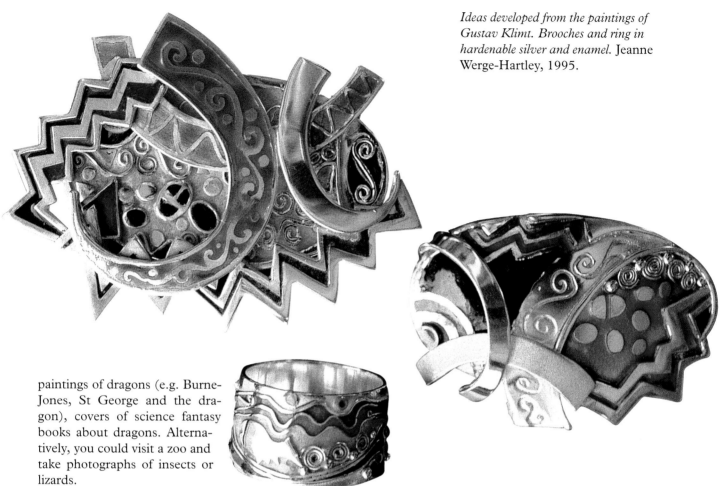

Ideas developed from the paintings of Gustav Klimt. Brooches and ring in hardenable silver and enamel. Jeanne Werge-Hartley, 1995.

paintings of dragons (e.g. Burne-Jones, St George and the dragon), covers of science fantasy books about dragons. Alternatively, you could visit a zoo and take photographs of insects or lizards.

Once you have collected lots of visual information, you may find that you start to see shapes and forms that could be starting points for a piece of jewellery. If so start to draw these shapes. If not try some of the following exercises:

1. Look at the images upside down – sometimes by looking at things in an unusual way abstract forms become more apparent, draw what you see.
2. Cut a small square or circle out of a piece of black paper and use it as a 'window' to isolate areas, again draw what you see.
3. Using a small mirror at right angles to the image look at what happens to elements when reflected along a line of symmetry, again draw the result.

4. Fold the image either once or several times, again draw the result.

Try these exercises with several images so that you have several possible ideas to develop further.

The next stage in the process is development. This is often the stage that people find the most difficult. This involves continually refining a shape or shapes by drawing it/them over and over again until you somehow arrive at a point that is 'right'. Again try these exercises with one of the ideas that has emerged out of the last stage.

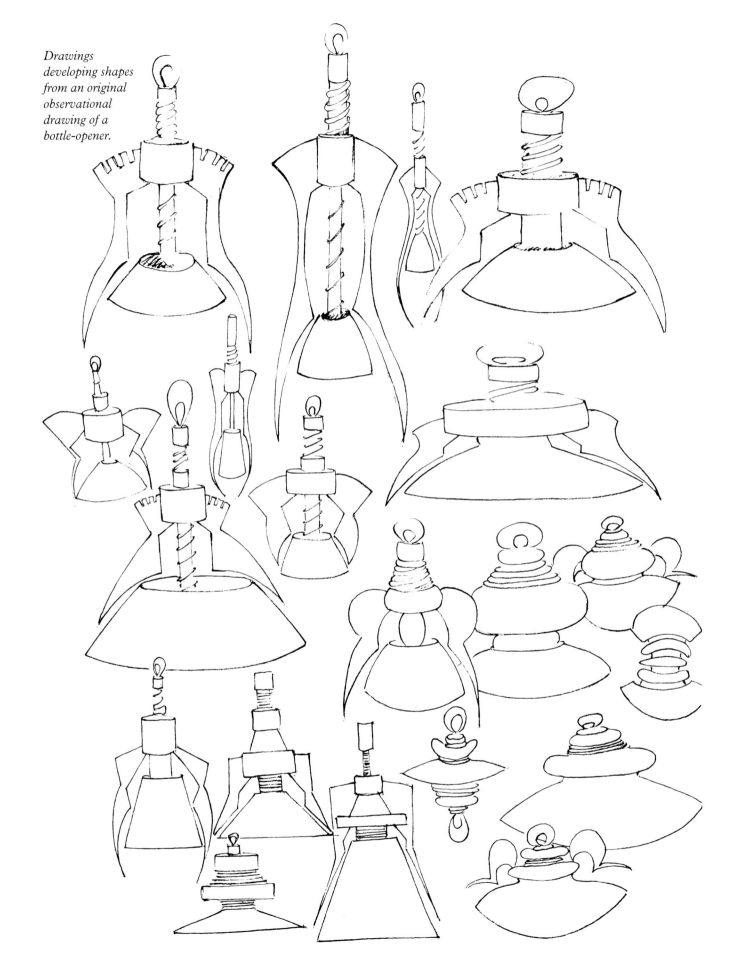

Drawings developing shapes from an original observational drawing of a bottle-opener.

Neckpieces, rings and brooch. Oxidized silver, 18kt yellow gold, blue glass, cubic zirconia stones and red resin. Catherine Hills, 1993, based on drawings of pebbles.

1. Do six drawings of the shape making it gradually fatter.
2. Do six drawings of the shape making it gradually thinner.
3. Do six drawings gradually stretching the shape.
4. Do six drawings gradually bending the shape.
5. Do six drawings changing the proportions, giving different emphasis to different elements of the form.
6. Do six drawings gradually making it sharper.
7. Do six drawings gradually making it softer.
8. Look at the negative shapes.
9. Turn it upside down.
10. Combine it with another form and start again with no. 1.

In the example on the previous page I have started by drawing an object from my kitchen, a bottle-opener. Using some of the exercises suggested I have played with the forms of the bottle-opener. Having done this I could now select some or part of the forms (it could be just a section of one of these forms) to develop through further drawing into a piece of jewellery.

Try not to judge the drawings as you are working on them. Wait until you have exhausted as many possibilities as you can and *then* look at what you have done (sometimes it is better to go and do something else for a while or leave the drawings until the next day). Choose a drawing that you feel is the most successful and draw it again, refining and improving it. The criterion is an individual internal one, you have to listen to yourself and feel your gut reaction to the ideas – for example, does that bit want to be heavier, longer, spikier, do you want the emphasis on this bit or that bit?

You may start to see ways in which you can interpret your idea in three dimensions or it may take more drawing to arrive at this point. Begin to think about what materials are appropriate to your idea, imagine what

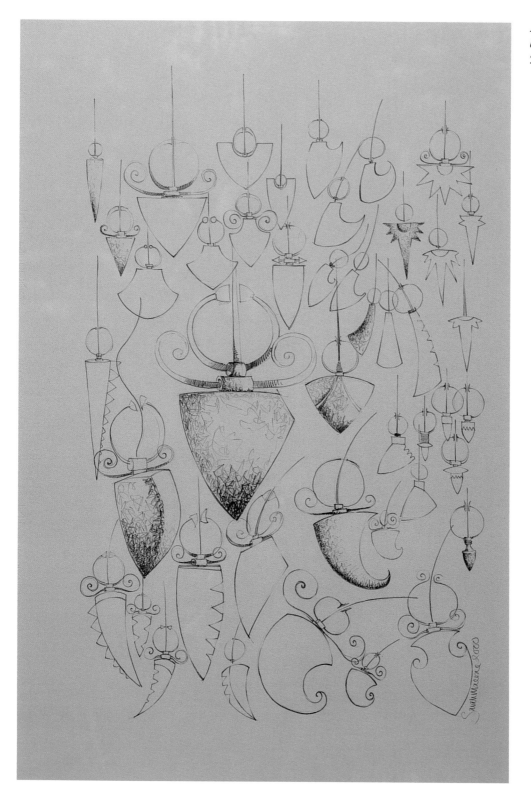

Drawings of penannular brooches. Sarah Macrae, 2000.

Tiara, soldered and twisted silver wire based on drawings of twigs.
Faith Chapman, 1998.

your idea could look like in metal, plastic, wood, paper or a combination of these. All materials have intrinsic qualities to which you need to be sensitive – for example, their weight, colour, strength, opacity and texture. A two-dimensional drawing can usually be interpreted in several different ways in three dimensions. To begin with, you are likely to be limited by your practical knowledge but gradually as you learn more processes and acquire experience working with more materials your range of choices will grow. Remember that to acquire any series of skills to a high level takes motivation, practice, patience and dedication, and we are all still struggling with those.

RECORDING YOUR WORK

Using a Camera

When you begin to make jewellery it is useful to also learn to record it. Although when you start it seems a long way off there may come a time when you are making things to exhibit or sell and it helps to have acquired enough photographic skills to keep a record of what you have made. Makers often need good quality slides for

sending to exhibition organizers or galleries and to have all your slides taken professionally is very expensive.

To get consistently good results you need an SLR camera with a macro lens, cable release and a tripod. If a macro lens is beyond your budget then close-up extension rings are an alternative. A standard lens on its own is not sufficient unless your work is really big as it will not focus close enough and the jewellery will appear as a tiny object in the middle of the slide, showing very little detail. It is better to take slides than prints as that is what you tend to need and if you do need prints then you can have a print taken from the slide or you can have the slides put onto a CD so that you can either view them on a computer screen or print them out.

It is best to work with the lowest ASA rated film you can. The lower the rating the slower the film and the finer the grain, which means a better quality image. Use 64 ASA daylight film if possible although if the weather is very overcast and the light levels are low you may need 200ASA.

Set the jewellery up on a neutral background, a mid-grey colour is best. If you use a white or black background the light meter in the camera registers mainly the background which means that the jewellery itself is either underexposed or over-exposed. The classic mistake people often make is to try to photograph jewellery on a black velvet background. The camera registers the black velvet, and the piece of jewellery is overexposed and bleaches out.

Use natural light and again for consistent results take photographs in good light but out of direct sunlight. If you decide to use artificial light you need to use a tungsten film that compensates for the more yellow light. Aim to have the aperture of the camera set on at least F8, the higher the number the greater the depth of field. That is the amount of depth that the camera can focus on. For example if you take a close up of a ring with the aperture set to F2.8 the front of the ring would be in focus but not the back, but the same shot at F8 or more will allow the whole ring to be in focus.

Having set the aperture adjust the speed of the shot. It is impossible to take a hand-held close-up shot at less than 1/60th of a second without the image blurring due to movement of the camera. Using a tripod and cable release there will not be a problem with camera shake and as the piece of jewellery will not move, the speed of the shot can be as slow as is necessary. So you have to balance the speed with the aperture to give you as much depth of field as possible – for example, 1/4 of a second at F8 is much better than 1/60th of a second at F2.8.

When adjusting the view of the jewellery through the viewfinder try to make it as large as possible in the frame, as this generally gives you the most detail and clearest results. The only exception is that sometimes rings can look like bangles if they are really large in the image, unless they have some sort of scale comparison. It would be helpful, in this case, to put a pin or something else of generally known dimensions in the shot to give an indication of size.

Check that nothing else is intruding into the shot, look carefully around the edges. Reflections are often a problem with highly polished surfaces and one way round this is to take the shot at a slight angle and ask someone to stand with a sheet of paper or cloth so that it is reflected in the metal.

Using Photocopiers and Scanners

If photography seems rather expensive or technically daunting another very effective way to record your work is to use a colour photocopier or a scanner and computer. Colour photocopiers will take surprisingly good copies of pieces of jewellery. They seem to have a depth of field of about an inch. Simply take your work to your local copier shop and place the jewellery face down on the copier with a piece of paper or cloth over the top (shutting the lid down is obviously not an option unless the work is very flat). If you have a computer and a scanner then it is even easier. Place your work face down on the bed of the scanner, cover with paper or cloth and scan. The advantage of using a scanner is that not only do you get a very clear image of the piece but it is exactly life-size. The only disadvantage is that if you want to keep the scanned image not just the print-out, the size of the file means that you can quickly use up large amounts of computer memory unless you have got a zip drive or CD writer to download onto.

Copyright

If you have your work recorded by a professional photographer it is important to discuss the copyright of the images. Some photographers sell you the copyright of the images and are happy for you to use them for whatever you want with only the proviso that you credit them for the work. Other photographers retain the copyright on their work and charge reproduction fees depending on how and where you want to use them.

LIST OF SUPPLIERS

UK SUPPLIERS

Acid-resist tape (1601 Scapa tape)

Gawler Tape & Plastics
24 Woodward Avenue
Westerleigh Business Park
Yate
Bristol BS37 5YS
Tel 01454 324265
Fax 01454 315158

Hadleigh Enterprises Ltd
Unit 11
Buckingham Square
Hurricane Way
Wickford
Essex SS11 8YQ
Tel 01268 572255

Local electronics suppliers
www.vikingtapes.co.uk

Acrylic

Technology Supplies Ltd
Phoenix Bank
Market Drayton
Shropshire TF9 1JS
Tel 01630 658185
Fax 01630 658185

Also try looking in your local Yellow Pages as many companies using plastics will often sell you offcuts.

Coloured copper wire

The Scientific Wire Company
18 Raven Road
London E18 1HW
Tel 020 8505 0002
Fax 020 8559 1114
www.wires.co.uk

Chemicals

Unfortunately the main chemical companies will not deal direct with members of the public. Find a friendly chemist who can order them for you. An independent chemist can sometimes be persuaded to make FM solution up for you. Alum (aluminium potassium sulphate) can be ordered from a chemist (it has a medical use, to treat foot odour). Sulphuric acid is usually available from hardware stores.

Clay (porcelain and Egyptian paste)

Potclays Ltd
Brickkiln Lane
Etruria
Stoke on Trent ST4 7BP
Tel 01782 219816
www.potclays.co.uk

Potterycrafts Ltd
Campbell Road
Shelton
Stoke on Trent ST4 4ET
Tel 01782 745000
www.potterycrafts.co.uk

Engineering supplies

Chronos Ltd
Unit 8 Executive Park
229–231 Hatfield Road
St Albans
Herts AL1 4TA
Tel 07974 353 185
Fax 01727 848130
email sales@chronos.ltd.uk
www.chronos.ltd.uk

Etching suppliers

Agate burnishers and etcher's varnish
L Cornelissen & Sons Ltd
105 Great Russell Street
London WC1B 3RY
Tel 020 7636 1045
Fax 020 7636 3655

Feathers

Handicrafts House
Silks Way
Warners Mill
South Street
Braintree
Essex CM7 3HA
Tel 01376 550099

Non-ferrous metals (copper, brass, etc.)

Rudgwick Metals Ltd
Church Street
Rudgwick
West Sussex RH12 3ED
Tel 01403 822471
email rudgwick@aol.com
www.rudgwickmetals.co.uk

Or look in your local directory for non-ferrous metal suppliers and also model shops who usually keep a stock of brass and copper sheet, tube and wire.

Paper

Paperchase
213 Tottenham Court Road
London W1P 9AF

Falkiner Fine Papers Ltd
76 Southampton Row
London WC1B 4AR
Tel 020 7831 1151
Fax 020 7430 1248

Precious metals

J Blundell and Sons Ltd
199 Wardour Street
London W1V 4JN
Tel 020 7437 4746
Fax 020 7734 0273

Cookson Precious Metal
43 Hatton Garden
London EC1N 8EE
www.cooksongold.com

D Pennellier & Co. Ltd
28 Hatton Garden
London EC1N 8DB

PMC (precious metal clay)

Silver Alchemy Marketing
2 Marshall Street
London W1F 9BB
Tel 020 8455 3132
Fax 020 8455 5296
email sales@silveralchemy.com
www.silveralchemy.com

Resin

Sculptors suppliers
Polyester resin technical booklets and tools

Alec Tiranti Ltd
70 High Street
Theale
Reading RG7 5AR
AND
27 Warren Street
London W1P 5DG

Slate

Local builders supplier, roofing slates

Steel

Surrey Stainless Steel Ltd
5 Sterling Way
Bedington Farm Road
Croydon CR0 4XN

Or look in your local directory for steel suppliers

Stones

Marcia Lanyon Ltd
PO Box 370
London W6 7ED
Tel 020 7602 2446
Fax 020 7602 0382

R. Holt & Co. Ltd
98 Hatton Garden
London EC1N 8NX
(sometimes have vegetable ivory)

Stone (English softstone, alabaster, soapstone, etc.)

Nigel Owen
42 High Street
Yelvertoft
Northants NN6 6LQ
Tel 01788 822281

Tools

Exchange Findings
49 Hatton Garden
London EC1N 8YS
www.cooksgold.com/trade-hatton.htm

Sutton Tools
37/38 Frederick Street
Birmingham B1 3HN
Tel 0121 236 7139
Fax 0120 236 4318

H.S. Walsh & Sons Ltd
12–16 Clerkenwell Road
London EC1M 5PQ

Wood (exotic hardwood)

Taylor & Sons Joinery
Unit 7, The Galleries
Fort Fareham
Newgate Lane
Fareham
Hampshire PO14 1AH
Tel/fax 01329 284390

US SUPPLIERS

Allcraft Tool and Supply
666 Pacific Street
Brooklyn
New York
NY 11217
Tel 001 800 645 7124
718 789 2800

Rio Grande Albuquerque
6901 Washington Avenue
NE Albuquerque
NM 87109
Tel 001 800 545 6566
www.riogrande.com

Frei and Borel
126 2nd Street
PO Box 796
Oakland
CA 94604
Tel 001 510 832 0355
www.ofrei.com

Gesswein
255 Hancock Avenue
Bridgeport
CT 06605
Tel 001 800 243 4466
www.gesswein.com

FURTHER READING

There have been many books published on the subject of jewellery both from a historical and technical point of view. I have listed here some of the books that I have found particularly helpful or inspirational.

HISTORICAL AND THEORETICAL

Broadhead, Caroline, *New Tradition and the Evolution of Jewellery 1966–1985* (The British Crafts Centre,1985)

Dormer, Peter, *The Art of the Maker* (Thames and Hudson,1994)

Dormer,Peter and Ralph Turner, *The New Jewellery Trends and Traditions* (Thames and Hudson, 1985)

Gere, Charlotte and Geoffrey C. Munn, *Artists Jewellery, PreRaphaelite to Arts and Crafts* (Antique Collectors, 1989)

Gilhooley, Derren and Simon Costin, *Contemporary British Jewellery Unclasped* (Black Dog Publishing, 1997)

Pullee, Caroline, *20th Century Jewellery* (The Apple Press, 1990)

Jewellery Redefined (1982) (exhibition Catalogue) (British Craft Centre)

TECHNICAL

Fisch, Arline M., *Textile Techniques in Metal for Jewellers, Sculptors and Textile Artists* (Van Nostrand Reinhold Company, 1975)

Hughes, Richard and Michael Rowe, *Colouring, Bronzing and Patination of Metals* (Watson Guptill, 1982)

McCreight, Tim, *The Complete Metalsmith: An illustrated Handbook* (Davis Publications, 1991)

McCreight, Tim, *Working with Precious Metal Clay* (Brynmorgen Press, 2000)

Midgley, Barry, *The Complete Guide to Sculpture Modeling and Ceramics* (North Light Books, 1982)

Alec Tiranti, *Technical Booklets* (*see* List of Suppliers)
  The Polyester Resin Booklet
  Soapstone, Broderick, Laurence
  Silicon Rubber

Untracht, Oppi, *Jewellery Concepts and Technology* (Robert Hale, 1982)

Wensley, Doug, *Pottery: a Manual of Techniques* (The Crowood Press, 1992)

INSPIRATIONAL

Fischer, Angela, *Africa Adorned* (Collins Publishers, 1984)

Game, Amanda and Elizabeth Goring, *Jewellery Moves* (exhibition Catalogue) (NMS Publishing, 1998)

Gerlach, Martin, *Primitive and Folk Jewellery* (Dover Publications, 1971)

Hovland, Rigmor and Sigurd Bronger, *Sigurd Bronger* (Labratorium Mechanum, Norway, 1998)

McCully, Marilyn, *Picasso Painter and Sculptor in Clay* (Academy of Arts, 1998) Particularly look at the pages of Picasso's sketchbooks where he is developing forms

Olver, Elizabeth, *Jewellery Design. The Artisans Reference Book* (North Light Books, 2000)

Young, Susan, *The Work of Angels* (British Museum Publications Ltd, 1989)

USEFUL ADDRESSES

UK ADDRESSES

The Crafts Council
44a Pentonville Road
Islington
London N1 9BY
Tel 020 7278 7700
Fax 020 7837 6891
www.craftscouncil.org.uk

Association for Contemporary Jewellery
PO Box 14
Hertford SG14 1WA
email acjorg14@hotmail.com

The Worshipful Company of Goldsmiths
Goldsmiths' Hall
Foster Lane
London EC2V 6BN

The London Assay Office
Goldsmiths Hall
Gutter Lane
London EC2V 8AQ
Tel 020 7814 9353
Fax 020 7814 9353

Designer Jewellers Group
22 Rivington Street
London EC2A 3DU
www.designerjewellersgroup.co.uk
www.johnmckellar.co.uk
www.emjewellery.co.uk
www.ddz.co.uk
www.facets.co.uk

The Edward James Foundation
West Dean College
West Dean
Nr Chichester PO18 0QZ
Tel 01243 811301
email westdean@pavilion.co.uk
www.westdean.org.uk

USA ADDRESSES

American Craft Council
72 Spring Street
New York
NY10012-4019
Tel 212/274-0630
www.craftcouncil.org

Society of North American Goldsmiths
(SNAG)
710 E. Ogden Avenue
Naperville
IL 60563-8603
Tel 630/579-3272
www.SNAGmetalsmith.org
www.PMCguild.com (precious metal clay website)

GLOSSARY

Anodizing
An electrolytic process used to create the illusion of colour on the surface of refractory metals (titanium, tantalum and niobium) and to create a layer that can be subsequently dyed on aluminium. The piece of metal suspended in a weak acidic solution becomes the anode in an electrical circuit.

Annealing
The process by which metal is made malleable through heating.

Assay
The testing of precious metal to determine the quality of the alloy.

Borax
The flux for silver soldering enabling solder to flow into a join.

Burnishing
The rubbing of a harder material (steel or agate) against a softer material (precious metal) to smooth and polish the surface.

Butt joint
Where two pieces of metal are joined edge to edge or end to end without overlapping and with little point of contact.

Capillary action soldering
The method of soldering used to join precious metal where a lower melting point alloy of the particular metal is used to make a virtually invisible join.

Chenier
Tubing.

Etching
The removal of metal by corrosion with acid.

Fibula
An ancient form of brooch formed from one continuous piece of metal similar to a safety pin.

Finding
The mechanical fixing on a piece of jewellery that enables it to function, e.g. ear wires.

Fire scale
The layer of flux and carbon that is left on the surface of metal after heating that is removed by pickling.

Firestain
A grey cloud of copper oxide that forms in the surface of standard silver when it is heated.

FM solution
A solution containing borax that acts as both a flux and a firestain inhibitor.

Forging
Using hammers to change the shape and section of a piece of metal. Precious metal is forged cold as it conducts heat very quickly. Steel and titanium can be forged hot as they retain heat.

Friction fit
Making two elements of a piece fit together through interlocking with each other so that they are held together by friction.

Granulation
A decorative technique used extensively by the ancient Etruscans using tiny grain (balls of precious metal).

Heat sink
Using a piece of metal or tweezers or spring tongs to draw heat away from a delicate area.

Lemel
Precious metal dust and scrap that is collected in the skin or tray of the workbench for recycling.

Oxidizing
The deliberate tarnishing of a piece by exposing the metal to a sulphur solution.

Pallions
The very small pieces that solder is cut into for capillary action soldering.

Patination
The colouring of the surface of metal by exposure to chemicals (*see* Further Reading list).

Pickling
The cleaning and removal of fire scale by immersion in sulphuric acid, Safety Pickle or alum.

Photoetching
A very accurate method of etching using photography to transfer a drawing onto the surface of the metal.

Penannular
Means broken circle and usually refers to an ancient form of brooch that incorporates a circle with a gap as a locking device.

Pre-soldering
Allowing the solder to run onto one surface by heating it, before placing it to join to another piece.

Quenching
The rapid cooling of a piece of metal by dropping into water.

Reticulation (Samorodok)
A decorative technique involving the controlled melting of the surface of metal.

Riveting
The mechanical fixing of two pieces of metal through the compressing along its length of a piece of wire that passes through holes drilled in the pieces to be joined.

Roller Printing
A decorative technique where a pattern is transferred to the surface of metal through pressure.

Vitrification
The point during firing at which clay becomes glass.

INDEX